Electrodics

Thieme Editions in Chemistry and Related Areas

Editors:

Kurt Niedenzu
Lexington, Kentucky

Hans Zimmer
Cincinnati, Ohio

 Georg Thieme Publishers Stuttgart

Electrodics

Modern Ideas Concerning Electrode
Reactions

By

Henry H. Bauer

Lexington, Kentucky

60 Figures, 10 Tables

A Halsted Press Book

1972

Georg Thieme Publishers Stuttgart
John Wiley & Sons New York - Toronto

Author:
Prof. Henry H. Bauer
Department of Chemistry
University of Kentucky
Lexington, Kentucky

Editors:
Prof. Kurt Niedenzu
Department of Chemistry
University of Kentucky
Lexington, Kentucky

Prof. Hans Zimmer
Department of Chemistry
University of Cincinnati
Cincinnati, Ohio

Published in the U.S.A. and Canada by Halsted Press, a Division of John Wiley & Sons, Inc.,
New York.

ISBN: 0 470-05920-6
Library of Congress Catalog Card No.: 72-7433

FOREWORD

With the present first volume of the "Thieme Editions in Chemistry" the publisher
and editors are beginning a series of treatises on various topics in chemistry and related
areas. The topics will be chosen in areas of contemporary interest and activity,
fields attracting increasing attention but which may not yet be familiar to non-special-
ists. Thus, interdisciplinary areas and those growing out of the classical areas of
chemistry will be stressed, as well as more classical topics where recent developments can usefully be brought to the attention of a wide audience to stimulate
applications and cross-fertilization of ideas. Every volume will present adequate
references in order to serve as a reliable guide to the frontiers of the subjects covered.

Electrochemistry is currently enjoying an increasing interest in areas such as synthe-
tic procedures, electrochemical aspects of membrane function and stimulation of
responses, and application of electroanalytical techniques to biological systems. Fuel
cells and battery systems are in process of development. It behooves the chemist
to be aware of these activities, and to acquire an understanding of the basic ideas
from which these developments arise.

The present book outlines the basic concepts in vogue in the study and elucidation
of electrodic reactions. While comprehensive, the treatise is concise and is intended
to permit the reader to obtain a broad view of work in electrodics in as short and
palatable a manner as possible.

It is hoped that this volume and later monographs in this series of "Thieme Editions
in Chemistry", will be useful to acquaint a general audience with the present state of
knowledge in selected topics as well as to stimulate the interest of the expert who
may find these monographs a useful reference. Moreover, it is hoped that the selection of the topics will permit their use as supplementary texts in advanced undergraduate and graduate classes in chemistry and the bordering disciplines.

Kurt Niedenzu   Hans Zimmer
Lexington, Kentucky   Cincinnati, Ohio

PREFACE

The stimulus for writing this book came from the lack of a text suited to the needs of students beginning graduate work in electrochemistry. It seemed desirable to have a book that would be fairly comprehensive, yet sufficiently concise and qualitative to be easily readable. It is my hope that this volume can serve that purpose and be useful to undergraduate students as a supplement to physical-chemistry texts, which almost entirely ignore mechanistic and kinetic aspects of electrode processes.

Topics that are fully and satisfactorily discussed elsewhere are covered here only to the extent that the reader might glean the chief principles involved, and the references given were chosen with the aim of providing suitable starting points for more extensive reading or searching of the literature. More discussion is devoted to areas that are not well covered in the existing literature, and the result is necessarily some unevenness in the depth of treatment of various topics as well as some reflection of the author's individual point of view.

Chapter 1 introduces general aspects of electrochemical systems, recalls the thermodynamic theory of galvanic cells, and discusses single-electrode potentials and processes; terms are defined, and the nomenclature used in relation to electrochemical methods is discussed. Chapter 2 is devoted to charge-transfer processes. Contemporary theories of charge transfer are reviewed, and the importance of other reaction-steps emphasized. Problems in the determination and interpretation of kinetic parameters for charge transfer are mentioned. Chapter 3 reviews facts and theories relating to the electrical double-layer, and discusses the influence of the double layer on electrochemical processes. In Chapter 4, aspects of mass transport are discussed with emphasis on diffusion and the role of mass transport in commonly employed techniques. Adsorption — other than that involved in setting up the double layer — is treated in Chapter 5, including a survey of the effects of surface-active substances on electrochemical reactions. Problems that arise in the use of solid electrodes are briefly discussed in Chapter 6. Finally, in Chapter 7, there are raised some points relevant to experimental measurements and the interpretation of results.

My thanks are due to the several people who provided criticisms of the original manuscript, to Ellen Nash and Jane Lane who were of great assistance with literature retrieval, and to Lucretia Reeves who typed several drafts of the manuscript.

I feel particularly fortunate in having had, as my scientific mentors, men who combined to a singular degree scientific achievement and outstanding personal qualities: Bruno Breyer, Philip Elving, and Thomas Iredale. Whatever virtues this book may possess are largely the result of their influence on my life and work.

Henry H. Bauer
Lexington, March 1971

TABLE OF CONTENTS

CHAPTER 1

Description of Electrochemical Systems

1.1 Two-Electrode Cells

1.1.1 Circuit for Electrochemical Work

Definitions of the scope of electrochemistry vary. Here, in order to define the topics that are to be discussed, it is useful to consider a simple electrochemical experiment. Such an experiment involves a chemical system whose electrical properties are of interest, usually a solution containing an electrolyte; at least two electrodes (most commonly of metal); and an electrical (polarizing and/or measuring) circuit, say a source of adjustable voltage and a current-measuring device (Fig. 1-1).

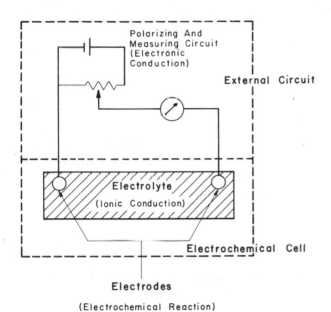

Fig. 1-1 A simple electrochemical circuit; differences in the mechanism of current flow in different parts of the circuit are indicated.

The flow of current in this circuit involves three distinct classes of phenomena:

(a)   In the electrical (measuring) circuit (commonly spoken of also as the "external circuit"), current flows by the conduction of electrons through metallic wires;

(b)   In the solution, current is carried by the movement of ions;

(c)   at the electrodes, reactions occur which form a "bridge" between the metallic conduction of electrons in the measuring circuit and the ionic conduction occurring in the solution; for instance, electrons may pass from the electrode to a substance in the solution, thereby reducing that substance.

The external circuit is present to permit the study of electrochemical processes, and the function of good experimental design is to ensure that current and voltage in the circuit will reflect phenomena occurring in the solution and at the electrodes rather than those in the external circuit. For instance, in cases where measurements involve the determination of current flow, it is desirable that the electrical resistance of the measuring circuit be negligible compared with that of the electrochemical cell, in order that the ratio of applied voltage to current flowing may reflect the resistance of the electrochemical cell rather than the combined resistances of circuit and cell.

The study of phenomena connected with the movement of ions in the electrolyte is conveniently termed *ionics*. Topics in this area are commonly dealt with in general courses in physical chemistry; such topics include the study of conductance, strong and weak electrolytes, activities, ionic mobilities, transport numbers, Debye-Hückel theory, and so on. These matters will not be treated in this book.

The study of reactions occurring at the electrodes is conveniently termed *electrodics*. This subject is commonly dealt with in physical-chemistry texts only from a thermodynamic point of view, which is helpful for the understanding of only a limited number of electrodic phenomena. Potentiometry, including pH measurement, and the ideal but not practical behavior of reversible cells as sources of power (batteries) can be understood on the basis of thermodynamic reasoning. However, such theory is of no help in situations where appreciable current flows, situations that include the majority of important applications of electrochemical studies. Moreover, no valid and useful answers can be given to questions such as: what characteristics of a system determine whether or not it will behave reversibly?

Questions such as this can be discussed only in terms of the mechanisms and rates of the reactions that take place. The main purpose of the present work is to introduce the reader to the salient points involved in such an approach. First, however, the thermodynamic treatment of reversible cells will be briefly reviewed.

1.1.2   Thermodynamic Results

In a cell such as that shown in Fig. 1-1, different reactions take place at the two electrodes. In general, at one electrode we have

$$aA + ne \rightleftarrows cC \tag{1-1}$$

(i.e., *a* molecules of A take up *n* electrons to form *c* molecules of C) while at the other electrode

$$bB - ne \rightleftarrows dD \tag{1-2}$$

The total reaction occurring in the cell is

$$aA + bB \rightleftarrows cC + dD \tag{1-3}$$

and the standard free energy of this reaction, $\Delta G°$, is related to the standard electromotive force, $E°$, by

$$\Delta G° = -nFE° \tag{1-4}$$

where F is the Faraday (ca. 96,500 coulombs). Under conditions other than the standard state, the voltage (E) of the cell is given by the Nernst equation

$$E = E° - (RT/nF) \ln (a_C^c a_D^d / a_A^a a_B^b) \tag{1-5}$$

where the a's are activities of the relevant species, R the universal gas constant, and T the absolute temperature. Derivation of these equations and their application is fully discussed in standard texts on physical chemistry; the signs of the terms containing potential (E, E°) in equations (1-4) and (1-5) are frequently shown as the opposite of those given above. The choice is governed by conventions, and a discussion of this matter can be found in a number of texts (e.g., reference 1).

Measurements of e.m.f. make available data on free-energy changes, entropies, and enthalpies; activity coefficients can be obtained as well as equilibrium constants and solubility products for a number of chemical reactions.

In these cases, the electrical measurements serve as a means of obtaining information about *chemical* processes (e.g., (1-3)). It is interesting to consider, however, whether one might also be able to obtain information about *electrochemical* reactions such as (1-1) and (1-2). One can, of course, write

$$E_{AC} = E°_{AC} - (RT/nF) \ln (a_C^c / a_A^a) \tag{1-6}$$

and

$$E_{BD} = E°_{BD} - (RT/nF) \ln (a_D^d / a_B^b) \tag{1-7}$$

This is compatible with eqn. (1-5), and one might therefore expect to be able to obtain thermodynamic information about the process that takes place at a single electrode. However, eqn.(1-5) differs from eqns. (1-6) and (1-7) in that the potentials in the former are measurable while those in the latter two cannot be measured. It is important to recall that tables of standard oxidation (or reduction) potentials for single-electrode processes are prepared by setting up a *convention* according to which the single-electrode standard potential of the H_2/H^+(aq) reaction is zero; this says nothing about an *absolute* difference of electrical potential between the electrode and the solution in a half-cell comprising a standard hydrogen electrode. The question of absolute single-electrode potentials is discussed below.

1.2 Processes at a Single Electrode

1.2.1 Single-Electrode Potentials

The possibility of measuring or calculating single-electrode potentials remains a matter of intermittent controversy. On the one hand, it is widely agreed that such potentials are not obtainable from calculations and experiments based solely on thermodynamic theories; and sometimes it is even said that such potentials have no physical significance or meaning and cannot be calculated. On the other hand, methods for measurement and/or calculation of single-electrode potentials continue to be proposed. This controversy is due to a lack of clarity about the concepts involved.

3

The potential difference, E, between two electrodes of a galvanic cell can be measured by means of a null-point potentiometric method or by means of a voltmeter (of sufficiently large internal resistance). It was recalled in Section 1.1.2 that this potential difference is related to the free energy of the chemical reaction taking place in the cell. Intuitively, then, one tends to feel that a single-electrode potential should reflect the free energy of the reaction occurring in the relevant half-cell and that there should again hold a relation of the type $\Delta G = -nFE'$ where E' is the "single-electrode potential." As mentioned in the previous section, however, such half-cell potentials E' differ from whole-cell e.m.f.'s, in that one cannot make an electrical measurement of a half-cell potential: any such measurement requires two leads to the measuring device, and one of these would necessarily go to the solution side of the half-cell, thereby forming a second electrode. Thus, the potential of a single electrode cannot be measured by the methods that are applicable to whole-cell voltages. Corollary to this is the fact that one cannot obtain the work equivalent of a single-electrode potential wholly as electrical energy. In other words, the relationship between chemical and electrical energies in a half-cell is quite different from that in a complete galvanic cell.

In a complete galvanic cell, the free energy of the chemical reactions is available as electrical work, and one could define the difference of electrical potential between the two electrodes on this basis. No such definition of electrode potential is available with a single electrode, and any valid definition of potential has to be made on some other basis.

An alternative definition is based on experience with potential differences in electrical circuits comprising conductors and resistors. Electrical potentials are defined on the basis of the work involved in moving "test charges", the test charge being an entity that does not interact with its environment chemically, or in any other "non-electrostatic" manner. Potential differences between two points in a conventional electrical circuit pose no problem of conception or measurement since the charge carriers are electrons, whose "chemical" or close-range interactions are the same at all points in the conductors comprising the electrical circuit in which potential differences are to be measured (assuming a single metal, usually copper, is used as conductor throughout). However, when one attempts to define a difference of electrical potential between two different phases, the problem of separating electrostatic and non-electrostatic (e.g., chemical) interactions arises, if one wishes to measure only one of these.

At first sight, such a separation might appear to be straightforward, but consideration of the nature of the forces involved shows that there is no acceptable existing definition of "chemical" and "electrical" that makes the separation possible; for example, van der Waals' forces, ion-dipole interactions, forces in adsorption, represent phenomena where a new definition would be required if separate contributions by "chemical" and by "electrical" interactions are to be conceived.

Thus, the attempt to conceive single-electrode potentials turns out to be impossible when essayed from a purely chemical viewpoint (electrical work equivalent of the free-energy change) as well as from a purely electrostatic viewpoint (test charges with no chemical interactions with the environment); and the impossibility resides precisely in

4

the fact that a half-cell is an entity whose chemical and electrical behavior is unique and therefore not definable on the basis of experience with other entities (galvanic cells or electrical circuits).

Since no use of test charges without chemical interactions is conceivable, calculations of "half-cell potentials" represent attempts to calculate (in volts) the free-energy change associated with a particular half-cell reaction. Because the result is expressed in electrical units, the implication could be drawn that this "voltage" is electrically measurable, or could be employed to perform electrical work. As pointed out earlier, such an implication is unwarranted. Consequently, it is important to bear in mind that calculated values of so-called "absolute" single-electrode potentials represent calculations of the free-energy change associated with a process such as

$$M_{(electrode)} \rightleftharpoons M^+_{(solution)} + e_{(electrode)} \qquad (1\text{-}8)$$

and that this potential is *not* an absolute *electrical* potential difference between the electrode and solution phases. In fact, existing definitions do not permit the use of the concept of an absolute electrical difference of potential between two phases; this matter has been treated fully by Parsons (2).

Unfortunately, this point is not clearly made in much of the existing literature; calculations and discussions of single-electrode potentials (3-6) are often couched in terms that do not clearly show that these are not electrical potential differences. Standard textbooks in physical chemistry often (7) mention the impossibility of measuring single-electrode potentials, but leave the impression that this is a *practical* difficulty and therefore the possibility of a calculation remains in the reader's mind. This is a very unfortunate manner of introducing the subject. Even an elementary treatment need not be couched in such terms (see reference 8); indeed, one can cover all the necessary areas using only cell e.m.f.'s (9). Single-electrode potentials are indeed convenient expressions in relation to tabulations of half-cell reactions, but it is not difficult to make clear that only an arithmetical operation and no physical significance is involved in the compilation and use of such tables.

Even more serious is the fact that books in the special area of electrochemistry often suffer from a lack of clarity on this issue, and in a number of cases could leave the misleading impression that somehow single-electrode potentials may be calculable or may even become determinable as purely electrical voltages. The correct view is of course given in good recent monographs (10); perhaps the most concise and clear discussion is that of Ives and Janz (11a).

To summarize: It is possible to define an *electrical* potential-difference only if that difference corresponds to the work done when an electrical test-charge is moved in absence of non-electrical interactions. This is not possible between an electrode and an electrolyte solution, so that a "half-cell potential" is not an electrical potential-difference.

1.2.2 Study of Single-Electrode Processes

The discussion in Section 1.2.1 should not be taken as an indication that no information is obtainable about the processes occurring at a single electrode: in fact, virtually all fundamental studies of electrode processes are carried out under conditions where the measured quantities are indicative of what is happening at one electrode.

It is not difficult to set up half-cells whose "potential", though unknown, remains constant under a wide variety of experimental conditions. For example, a half-cell in which the reaction

$$H^+_{(aq)} + e \leftrightarrows 1/2 \, H_{2 \, (gas)} \tag{1-9}$$

occurs reversibly at unit activity of $H^+_{(aq)}$ and 1 atmosphere of pressure of hydrogen gas can be made using a platinized platinum electrode. *Changes* of potential in any other half-cell can be measured by noting the change of e.m.f. of the whole cell consisting of the "unknown" half-cell and the (reference) hydrogen-electrode half-cell. The latter is used by convention as the zero point of the scale of half-cell potentials; this does not, of course, mean that the "absolute" potential of the hydrogen electrode is zero, but merely that half-cell potentials determined on this scale enable one to calculate the e.m.f. of a galvanic cell composed of any combination of two half-cells whose "potentials" are known with reference to the hydrogen-electrode potential.

In practice, other half-cells are more commonly used because of greater operational convenience: for instance, a calomel electrode containing mercury, mercurous chloride, and chloride ion at a specified concentration; or a silver – (silver-chloride) electrode containing chloride ion at a specified concentration. Reference electrodes are authoritatively discussed in a classic monograph (11).

Since most experiments are not carried out under potentiometric conditions, but rather under conditions where appreciable current flows, it is vitally necessary that reference electrodes should not change in potential at the levels of current flow involved. This can be achieved (see Section 2.2.3), and one can then observe the relation between current and change of potential at an electrode that is coupled to a reference half-cell to form a complete electrochemical cell.

When changes of current level produce no variation of the potential of the reference half-cell, the latter behaves as if its resistance to current flow were zero (at any rate, negligible). Therefore, the magnitude of the current is determined by the reactions taking place at the other electrode, and we are in a position to study these reactions in terms of the relation between current and changes of potential; the reference electrode exerts no influence on either of these quantities (except, in some cases, as a result of changes in liquid-junction potentials: see Section 7.4.1).

Often, for instance in polarographic work, one uses (instead of a true reference-electrode) an electrode whose area is very large compared to that of the indicator electrode. The magnitude of the current is then determined only by what happens at the small electrode – in the same way as the flow of a fluid in a pipe is limited not by the characteristics of sections of pipe with large cross-section, but by the nature of valves or other constrictions whose cross-sections are sufficiently smaller.

Thus, the nature of processes at single electrodes is readily studied; the conceptual difficulties associated with "absolute single-electrode potentials" are irrelevant in this respect. In the remainder of this book – except where otherwise indicated – we will be concerned only with the phenomena occurring at a single electrode. Thus, when we speak of "the" electrochemical reaction, it will signify the reaction at one electrode.

1.3 Terms and Definitions

1.3.1 General

In a galvanic cell, charge transfer between electrode and solution occurs in opposite senses at the two electrodes. At the cathode, electrons move in the electrode towards the electrode-solution interface and negative charge is transferred into the solution (or positive charge from solution to electrode); thus, a *cathodic reaction or process* is one that involves reduction of a species in the solution. A *cathodic potential* is one that aids reduction, and as an electrode potential is made more cathodic, reduction takes place more readily. Similarly, at the *anode,* an oxidation takes place (*anodic reaction*), more readily the more anodic the potential.

Commonly, experiments are carried out in such a way that only processes occurring at one of the electrodes determines the behavior of the cell. That electrode is then called an *indicator* or *working* electrode; very frequently, it is of physically small size, a *microelectrode.* When the term "microelectrode" is used, it is generally understood that this is an indicator or working electrode.

A *reference electrode* is one that maintains a constant potential; changes in cell e.m.f. then reflect changes in the potential of the working electrode when the second electrode is a reference electrode. Sometimes, a third electrode is used for the purpose of carrying much of the current in order that only a small or negligible current has to pass through the reference electrode; such an additional electrode is called a *counter electrode.* The function of a counter electrode is discussed in Section 7.4.2.

The current flowing in an electrochemical cell may arise from a charge-transfer process at an electrode, whereby a reaction occurs in proportion to the amount of electricity involved. Such reactions follow Faraday's laws of electrolysis – e.g., reduction of Fe(III) ions to Fe(II), deposition of a metal, evolution of a gas, and so on. Current flowing as the result of such a process is termed *faradaic current.* Current arising from other types of processes is called *non-faradaic.* When no charge transfer can occur, application of a potential to an electrode will attract ions of one charge-sign and these will move to the electrode, and a corresponding amount of electronic charge moves in the external circuit (into or out of the electrode) i.e. a current flows but no charges cross the electrode-solution interface; after a time, the current ceases – when the electrode is in a state of equilibrium of charge. The current that flows during the charging process is *non-faradaic;* it is frequently called the *charging current.* Since the ability of an electrode to hold charge is analogous to the behavior of an electrical condenser or capacitor, the charging current is often called the *capacitive* or *capacitative* current.

Often, the system studied contains a small amount of reducible or oxidizable material – the *electroactive species* – and a large amount of an "inert" species, i.e. one that is

7

not oxidizable or reducible under the conditions used. This *inert electrolyte* is usually called the *supporting electrolyte* or the *background electrolyte.*

Electrochemical systems have long been classified according to their *reversibility.* Many galvanic cells can convert chemical into electrical energy with virtually complete efficiency, indicating that the reactions involved proceed in a way that satisfies the criterion of thermodynamic reversibility — viz., that equilibrium is maintained at all times. Thus, one can change the voltage of the cell slightly, and then return it to its original state by changing the voltage back again. A *reversible cell* follows the Nernst equation, which has been derived for a thermodynamically reversible system. A reversible electrode process, then, is one that follows Nernstian behavior. On the other hand, there are cells that do not follow Nernstian behavior: these are *irreversible,* and at least one of the electrode processes occurring is *irreversible.* Frequently, the e.m.f. of an irreversible cell cannot be measured because it does not maintain a constant value.

This usage of the terms *reversible* and *irreversible* is classical, and continues. However, it is now known that the "reversibility" of a cell or of a redox system or of an electrode depends on the experimental conditions. Thus, a cell may behave reversibly in potentiometric measurements but irreversibly in polarographic studies; or, a system may be reversible when studied under alternating voltages of low frequency and irreversible at higher frequencies. Therefore, "reversibility" is not an inherent property of a cell — it is a type of behavior; and it is better to speak of a system *behaving* reversibly or irreversibly, rather than *being* reversible or irreversible. In Section 2.2.3, it will be shown that a kinetic theory of charge transfer enables one to understand why a given system might behave reversibly or irreversibly under different experimental conditions.

A reversible electrode is, by definition, at equilibrium and its potential is an equilibrium potential. When the potential changes from its equilibrium value, the change is called the *overvoltage* (occasionally, one sees the term *overpotential* in this connection). The presence of an overvoltage indicates irreversible behavior, and we use the term *polarization* to describe the state that leads to irreversibility and the appearance of an overvoltage. In this condition, the electrode or cell is *polarized.* When the state of polarization is removed, the process responsible is one of *depolarization:* the electrode is thereby *depolarized.* If the presence of a particular substance causes depolarization, that substance is a *depolarizer.*

A completely reversible electrode would maintain its equilibrium potential under all circumstances. For example, no matter how large a current is passed, no change of potential occurs — the electrode behaves as if it had zero resistance. Such an electrode is *non-polarizable.* In practice, one finds electrodes whose behavior approaches non-polarizability provided not too large a current is passed, and these make the best reference electrodes.

By contrast, when an electrode is polarized, it behaves as if it had a large resistance. Then, an increase in applied potential produces little, if any, increase in current flow; this behavior is often used as a criterion for the state of polarization (when a system

8

behaves in this way, it is consequently termed polarized). An *ideally polarized electrode* is one whose resistance to charge transfer is infinite; no faradaic current can pass such an electrode (though non-faradaic current can) because charges cannot be transferred across the electrode-solution interface.

Many phenomena can contribute to a state of polarization. If (slow) movement of the electroactive species is the cause, we speak of *concentration polarization;* if a (slow) chemical reaction is the hindrance, we have *reaction polarization;* if the charge-transfer process itself is responsible, there exists *activation polarization.*

These descriptions and definitions cover common usage and the present author's preferences; there is no real uniformity in the literature on many of these terms. For instance, the length of useful life of dry cells is limited by the occurrence of chemical changes near the electrodes; substances incorporated during manufacture to minimize or slow down these changes are termed depolarizers, whereas in polarographic work, it is usual to speak of any reducible or oxidizable species as a depolarizer. While both usages are reasonably compatible with that given above (decreasing a state of polarization permits added current flow without a change of potential), the usages are rather more specific.

1.3.2 Potential, Voltage, and Tension

"Potential" is a widely used term in electrochemistry as well as in electrostatics. The discussion in Section 1.2.1 demonstrates how errors of understanding can result from the use of the term "potential" if one is not clear as to whether an *electrical* potential is under consideration, or an electrochemical or chemical potential. Further, use of the term "electrode potential" can lead to the mistaken idea of an "absolute" (electrical) single-electrode potential since the term does not clearly show that the quantity referred to is usually the *difference of electrical potential* between the electrode in question and a hydrogen reference-electrode.

For these and similar reasons, the recommendation has been made (12, 13) that a new terminology be introduced using the terms chemical, electrochemical, and electric *tensions,* with the same connotation as the French *"tension"* and the German *"Spannung".* This terminology has been adopted by *Electroanalytical Abstracts* and by a few individual workers, including some writers of textbooks (14). However, there is also opposition to this terminology, and the present author does not believe that it will come into general use in English. It can be extremely awkward (e.g., "surface electric tension" for "surface potential"), and well-known words are replaced by strange new ones ("tensiometry" for "potentiometry"). The terminology of "tensions" will therefore not be used in this book; details of that terminology, as well as a very useful discussion of fundamental concepts in electrochemistry, are given by van Rysselberghe (13).

The term "voltage" is also in common usage. It seems, however, that no explicit attention has been given to the way in which the term should or might be used. It is clearly a quantity applicable only to electrical magnitudes (i.e., expressed in volts), and consistent usage in this way could meet some of the objections raised to the manner in which "potential" is used by electrochemists. Some authors use "potential" and "voltage" as a way of distinguishing the potential of an electrode (relative to a reference electrode, but usually assuming the absence of liquid-junction potentials, ohmic drop, or other "artefacts") from the cell voltage (potential drop across the electrochemical cell, including ohmic drop, liquid-junction potentials and so on); so, for instance, one can distinguish (15) between methods in which the electrode potential is controlled ("potentiostatic") and those where the cell voltage is controlled ("voltostatic").

In practice, however, there is no uniformity of usage amongst electrochemists. "Potential" and "voltage" were frequently used interchangeably, and now we have "tension", "potential", and "voltage" all used by various authors.

1.3.3 Electrochemical Methods

Electrochemical methods have been named partly in a systematic way and partly for historical reasons. Attempts at completely systematic classification and nomenclature have been published (16, 17) but these are not entirely successful and some common usage is in conflict with them.

Systematic classification and nomenclature is based on the type of measurement made, and on the experimental conditions used. Frequently, one controls the electrode potential, or the cell current, or the charge injected onto an electrode: one then speaks of *controlled potential* (or *potentiostatic)* methods, of *controlled current* (or *galvanostatic*) methods, and of *coulostatic* methods respectively. This terminology is not entirely logical since "static" conveys the idea of a "constant" rather than of a "controlled" variable.

More specific nomenclature includes reference to the variable being measured: *conductometry* refers to the measurement of conductance, *potentiometry* to the measurement of electrode potentials. In these cases, other factors (e.g. time) are not normally of significance. In other cases, more than one variable is of importance, and the terminology reflects that: *chronoamperometry* for the measurement of current as a function of time, *chronopotentiometry* for the measurement of potential as a function of time.

A complete description refers to both the controlled and the measured variables: *linear-sweep chronoamperometry* describes the measurement of the current as a function of time when the potential is increased (swept) linearly with time, rather than in a situation where the potential is constant or varies perodically.

There are, however, non-systematic but time-honored terms that are not only in common use but also have the advantage of being single words rather than a combination of two or more terms. The classical example is *polarography*, describing current-vs.-potential behavior at an electrode where concentration polarization subsists (or can be made to subsist). This technique was discovered and named by Heyrovsky in the early 1920's. His work was carried out with a dropping mercury electrode, and in more recent years it has become fashionable, especially in the U.S.A., to use the term *polarography* only for work with mercury electrodes; the same technique applied to other electrodes is called *voltammetry*. This usage arose from an article (18) published in 1940, and is now widely accepted. Both terms refer by definition to a situation where only one electrode controls the flow of current; almost invariably, there is present a supporting electrolyte at a concentration considerably in excess (say 50-fold greater than) the concentration of the electroactive species.

In relatively recent years, a number of variations of the polarographic technique have been introduced. In the classical technique, the electrode potential is essentially constant while the current is being measured — the slow change of potential while a polarogram is recorded has no influence on the measured magnitude of the current. This is not the case in the techniques defined below:

Oscilloscopic or *oscillographic polarography* (19) refers to methods where the electrode potential changes rapidly with time, it may be linearly, sinusoidally, or in some other way. The current is observed by use of an oscilloscope since its magnitude varies too rapidly to permit the use of other recording devices whose response time is slower.

Alternating current (a.c.) polarography (20) is a method in which an alternating voltage of small amplitude (millivolts or tens of millivolts) is superposed on the direct polarizing potential; the alternating current is measured. The superposed alternating voltage is usually of sinusoidal shape. When, instead, it has a square-wave form, one speaks of *square-wave polarography* (21), and in this method the current is usually measured by "sampling" at short intervals of time during each cycle of the square wave. In *radio-frequency polarography* (22), the rectification produced by a radio-frequency alternating voltage is measured. In *pulse polarography* (23), voltage pulses of amplitude of the order of tens or hundreds of millivolts are superposed on the direct polarizing potential.

Tensammetry (20) is a useful term for the study of adsorption-desorption processes using the same apparatus as in a.c. polarography.

The systematic classifications by Delahay et al. (16) and by Reilley and Murray (17) should be consulted for detailed discussion of the nomenclature of electrochemical methods. It must be remembered, however, that there are variations of usage between different workers in the field.

1.4   References

1. K.J.Vetter, *Electrochemical Kinetics* (Academic Press, 1967)
2. R.Parsons, *Modern Aspects of Electrochemistry (no. 1)*, (Butterworths 1954) p. 103
3. H. Strehlow, *Z. Elektrochem., 56* (1952) 119
4. M. Salomon, C.G. Enke, and B.E. Conway, *J. Chem. Phys., 43* (1965) 3989
5. M. Salomon, *J. Electrochem. Soc., 113* (1966) 940
6. I. Oppenheim, *J. Phys. Chem., 68* (1964) 2959
7. For example: G.M. Barrows, *Physical Chemistry* (McGraw-Hill 1961) p. 596; H.D.Crockford and S.B.Knight, *Fundamentals of Physical Chemistry,* 2nd ed. (Wiley 1964) p. 254; G.H.Duffey, *Physical Chemistry* (McGraw-Hill 1962) p. 401; W.H.Hamill, R.R.Williams and C.MacKay, *Principles of Physical Chemistry,* 2nd ed. (Prentice-Hall 1966) p. 253; S.H.Maron and C.F.Prutton, *Principles of Physical Chemistry* (MacMillan 1958) pp. 518, 524.
8. For example; E. Hutchinson, *Physical Chemistry* (Saunders 1962) p. 259; W.J.Moore, *Physical Chemistry,* 3rd ed. (Prentice-Hall 1962) p. 390

9. D.F. Eggers, N.W.Gregory, G.D.Halsey, and B.S.Rabinovitch, *Physical Chemistry* (Wiley 1963) pp. 378-386

10. W.M.Clark, *Oxidation-Reduction Potentials of Organic Systems* (Williams and Wilkins 1960) pp. 21, 113; G. Kortum, *Treatise on Electrochemistry* (Elsevier 1965) p. 305; K.J. Vetter, *Electrochemical Kinetics* (Academic Press 1967) p. 97 ff.

11. D.J.G. Ives and G.J.Janz, *Reference Electrodes* (Academic Press 1961); (a)-Chapter I, Section II

12. P. van Rysselberghe, *Electrochim. Acta, 3* (1961) 257

13. P. van Rysselberghe, *Electrochim. Acta, 9* (1964) 1343.

14. A.J. de Bethune, *Encyclopedia of Electrochemistry* (Reinhold 1964); E.Hutchinson, *Physical Chemistry* (Saunders 1962)

15. W.H.Reinmuth, *Anal. Chem., 36* (1964) 211R

16. P. Delahay, G. Charlot and H.A. Laitinen, *Anal. Chem., 32* (May 1960) 103A

17. C.N.Reilley and R.W.Murray, *Treatise on Analytical Chemistry Part I, Vol. 4* (Interscience 1963) Ch. 43.

18. I.M.Kolthoff and H.A. Laitinen, *Science, 92* (1940) 152

19. J.Heyrovsky and J. Kuta, *Principles of Polarography* (Czechoslovak Academy of Sciences, Prague 1965) Ch. XXII

20. B.Breyer and H.H. Bauer, *Alternating Current Polarography and Tensammetry* (Wiley 1963)

21. G.C.Barker and I.L.Jenkins, *Analyst, 77* (1952) 685

22. G.C.Barker, *Anal. Chim. Acta, 18* (1958) 118

23. G.C.Barker and A.W.Gardner, *Z. Anal. Chem., 173* (1960) 79

CHAPTER 2

Electrode Reactions

2.1 The Overall Electrochemical Reaction

All electrochemical changes by definition involve both chemical and electrical changes. These changes can be regarded as occurring in a single reaction, e.g. the reduction of a metal ion with incorporation of the resulting atom into a deposit on the electrode; however, in attempting to understand the characteristics of electrode processes, it is necessary to consider the mechanism in considerably more detail.

Electrode reactions are heterogeneous: the charge-transfer step takes place at the electrode-solution interface. Obviously, the electroactive species must come to the interface, and the product(s) of the reaction will usually move away. Thus, the transport of electroactive material by processes such as convection, electrical migration, and/or diffusion will form part of the overall reaction. In some cases, formation of crystals and incorporation of deposited material into a lattice will be involved. There may also be adsorption processes involving reactant and/or product; chemical reactions of the usual type, such as the association and dissociation of complexes, acid-base reactions (addition of protons to reactant and/or product, or removal of protons), unusual chemical reactions such as partial or total dehydration of ions; as well as others.

As a result, electrochemical reactions can be quite complicated, and frequently are in practice. Observed phenomena may be determined chiefly by the charge-transfer step itself or by some other step in the overall sequence.

It is not feasible to give here a detailed and general account of the influences of various reaction-steps since different processes involve quite different mechanisms. Numerous theoretical discussions have been published dealing with particular types of processes: reactions preceding and/or following charge transfer, adsorption of reactant and/or product, catalysis by the product or by some other substance, and so on. These discussions are limited not only to particular types of reaction, but frequently also concern particular experimental conditions, i.e., how a particular reaction will behave when examined by a particular technique. This material will be discussed only in a general and qualitative way for the purposes of the present context.

As in any reaction, the net rate of an electrochemical process is determined by the rate of the slowest step in the whole sequence of reactions. If this happens to be the charge-transfer step, then the latter can be readily studied; if the slowest step is a chemical reaction, then its rate is determinable. If two or more steps are of comparable rate and so slow as to limit the overall rate, analysis may be complicated: the results need to be fitted to a theoretical model describing the combined influence of the various rate-determining steps.

Here, characteristics of various types of reaction steps will be discussed separately. The charge-transfer step, which is always present, is treated in Section 2.2. The influence of the environment (at the surface of the electrode) on charge transfer is discussed in Section 3.6. Mass transport is dealt with in Chapter 4, various aspects of adsorption processes in Chapter 5, and crystallization and electrocatalysis in Sections 6.4 and 6.5.

2.2   The Charge-Transfer Step

2.2.1 Definition of the Charge-Transfer Step

It is not easy to define precisely what part of an electrochemical reaction is actually "the charge-transfer step". Reactions such as mass transport and adsorption are commonly regarded as separate steps, as are chemical reactions such as the addition or loss of protons. In the hydrogen-evolution reaction, hydrogen atoms (adsorbed on the electrode) are regarded as viable chemical species to the extent that they are taken to be the product or reactant in the charge-transfer step. In the reduction of metal complexes, a change in coordination number is sometimes taken to be a separate step preceding reduction, but in other cases not.

An essential part of the uncertainty in such a definition is due to the fact that it depends on our state of understanding: if it is known that the reducible species is, e.g., a complex of coordination number different from that found in the bulk of the solution, then dissociation of the complex will be regarded as a separate step preceding reduction; in absence of this knowledge, no such steps would be postulated and the results probably analyzed on the basis that the fate of the ligands is determined within the charge-transfer step itself. Thus, in the reduction of hydrated cations, the process of dehydration is commonly taken to be part of the charge-transfer step since no independent information on the role of dehydration in the reaction is presently available.*

The difference in electrical potential between the bulk of the solution and the solution side of the interface may affect the energy state of the reactant as well as its rate of movement to the surface. Usually such effects are considered as a part of the charge-transfer step, but sometimes they are considered in terms of the influence on mass transport (see Section 3.6).

Thus, "the charge-transfer step" is not as precise a concept as may appear at first sight. Other aspects of this question are important in the discussion of modern theories of charge transfer where attempts are made at *a priori* calculations of energies and rates involved in the charge-transfer process (see Section 2.2.5).

---

*However, dehydration as a separate (kinetically controlling or at least kinetically important) step has been postulated on theoretical grounds in a number of cases. Experimental evidence for kinetic control of an overall electrochemical reaction by a dehydration step has been presented by Gierst and Hurwitz (1) and Shirai (2) in the reduction of nickel (II), by von Sturm and Ressel (3) in the reduction of zinc (II), and by Woodburn et al. (4) and Hawkridge and Bauer (5) in the reduction of copper (II).

2.2.2 Kinetic Treatment

Much experimental work has been done with systems in which appreciable current flows. Often, the current is found to vary exponentially with the applied voltage, and this empirical evidence is summarized by the Tafel equation

$$\eta = a \pm b \log |i| \tag{2-1}$$

where η is the overvoltage, i the current and a and b are constants (b is often called the *Tafel slope*); the sign of the second term changes according to whether the process is anodic or cathodic, and depends on the sign convention used for η.

The Tafel equation holds for a great number of systems over a wide range of overvoltages; typically, however, it breaks down at low values of the overvoltage where comparatively little current flows (Fig. 2-1).

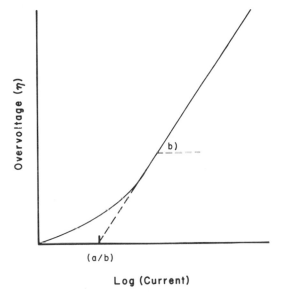

Fig. 2-1 Schematic Tafel plot showing deviation from linearity at low overvoltages and significance of the parameters *a* and *b*.

Attempts to formulate a kinetic theory of electrode processes began with the empirically based assumption that the Tafel equation is widely applicable. Since the range of validity is at higher rather than lower overvoltages, it seemed reasonable to infer that the Tafel law does not deal with equilibrium situations but, rather, represents the relationship between current and voltage for a uni-directional electrode process, i.e. a situation where oxidation or reduction is occurring with a negligible contribution from re-reduction or re-oxidation respectively.

It seems, then, that the rate of an electrochemical reaction (which is directly proportional to the magnitude of the current) is an exponential function of the electrode potential; from the Tafel equation above,

$$i = \exp[-a/b]\exp[\eta/b] \tag{2-2}$$

15

for a uni-directional process. A general theory, however, requires that one consider the situation in which both forward and backward reactions can in principle occur. Thus, we want to consider the reaction

$$O + ne \rightleftharpoons R \tag{2-3}$$

where O represents a molecule of the oxidized species and R represents a molecule of the reduced species, these species differing by n electrons.

The forward and backward reactions can be described by rate constants, k_f and k_b respectively. The rates of the forward and backward reactions are then given by the products of these rate constants and the relevant concentrations, the rate of the forward reaction being $k_f C_o$, and of the backward reaction $k_b C_R$; C_o and C_R are the concentrations of O and R at the electrode surface. These rates can be expressed in terms of currents for the forward and backward reactions, i_f and i_b respectively;

$$i_f = nFAk_f C_o \tag{2-4}$$

$$i_b = nFAk_b C_R \tag{2-5}$$

where A is the area of the electrode* and F the Faraday. (Quite often, the *current density*, i/A, is used rather than the actual magnitude of the current; frequently, the same symbol "i" is used for current density).

These formulations merely represent an application of the law of mass action to forward and backward processes, both considered to be of first order; the role of the electrons in the process is considered by assuming that the magnitudes of the rate constants depend on the electrode potential. Usually, this dependence is described by assuming that a fraction, αE, of the electrode potential is effective in facilitating the reduction process, while the remaining fraction of the potential, $(1-\alpha)E$, is effective in making more difficult the (re)oxidation. This idea is expressed by the equations

$$k_f = k_f^\circ \exp[-\alpha nFE/RT] \tag{2-6}$$

$$k_b = k_b^\circ \exp[(1-\alpha)nFE/RT] \tag{2-7}$$

where α is called the *transfer coefficient* and E is the electrode potential relative to a suitable reference potential (some authors use the *symmetry factor, β*, instead of α in these equations). The assumption embodied in equations (2-6) and (2-7) is discussed in Section 2.2.4.

Equations (2-6) and (2-7) are compatible both with the Nernst equation for equilibrium conditions and with the Tafel law for uni-directional processes, as will be shown in the following.

Equations (2-4) and (2-5) embody the usually made and, at first sight, trivial assumption that the current is directly proportional to the available surface area of the electrode. However, it may happen that the current density varies at different parts of the surface, and in that case the total current may not be directly proportional to the total area. Variation of current density may result from a particular geometrical arrangement of the electrodes – e.g., at a disc-shaped working electrode (6), the total current may be proportional to the radius (r) of the disc, rather than to the area (πr^2). Another aspect of this effect, in connection with a.c. measurement, is discussed in Section 7.3.5.

16

Under equilibrium conditions, no net current flows, and

$$i_f = i_b = i_o \tag{2-8}$$

where i_o is the *exchange current*. Using the equation (2-4) to (2-8),

$$C_o k_f^o \exp[-\alpha nFE/RT] = C_R k_b^o \exp[(1-\alpha)nFE/RT] \tag{2-9}$$

so that

$$E = (RT/nF)\ln(k_f^o/k_b^o) + (RT/nF)\ln(C_o/C_R) \tag{2-10}$$

The *formal standard potential* E_C^o (concentrations rather than activities are considered) is defined by $C_o = C_R$, so that

$$E_C^o = (RT/nF)\ln(k_f^o/k_b^o) \tag{2-11}$$

If the formal standard potential is taken as the reference point of the potential scale, as is convenient with reversibly occurring processes (i.e., if we set $E_C^o = 0$),

$$k_f^o = k_b^o = k \tag{2-12}$$

where k is called the *(standard heterogeneous) rate constant* of the charge-transfer step; frequently, the symbols k_s, k_h, or $k_{s,h}$ are used in this connection. Combining equations (2-10) and (2-11) yields

$$E = E_C^o + (RT/nF)\ln(C_o C_R) \tag{2-13}$$

which is the Nernst equation written in terms of concentrations rather than activities. Therefore, the kinetic treatment given above is, for equilibrium conditions, compatible with the known facts and with thermodynamic theory.

The exchange current is a useful parameter. It can be written in a convenient form by using equations (2-4), (2-6), (2-10) and (2-12):

$$i_o = nFA\, k C_o^{(1-\alpha)} C_R^\alpha \tag{2-14}$$

The exchange current is a measure of the kinetics of the system at any equilibrium potential; it describes the lability of the equilibrium, the rate of exchange of charges between oxidized and reduced reactant without net overall change (oxidation or reduction). The dependence of the exchange current on potential is determined by the manner in which changes of C_O and/or C_R influence the electrode potential (or *vice versa*).

The standard rate-constant, k, on the other hand has been defined for a particular potential — the formal standard potential of the system — and is not in itself sufficient to characterize the system unless the transfer coefficient is also known.

The relationship between the current for the forward process, the current for the backward process, and electrode potential is illustrated in Figure 2-2.

It has just been shown that the Nernst relationship results from equations (2-6) and (2-7) for equilibrium conditions, where the net current is zero. It can be seen that when the potential is sufficiently different from the equilibrium potential (i.e. for sufficiently large overvoltages), the net current becomes equal in magnitude to the forward current (or, for anodic overvoltages, to the backward current). Then, one can write

$$i = nFA\, k\, C_O \exp[-\alpha nF\eta/RT] \tag{2-15}$$

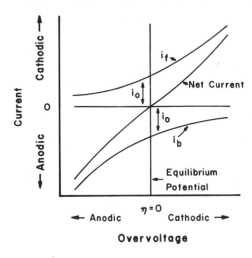

Fig. 2-2 Relationship between overvoltage and cathodic, anodic, and net currents.

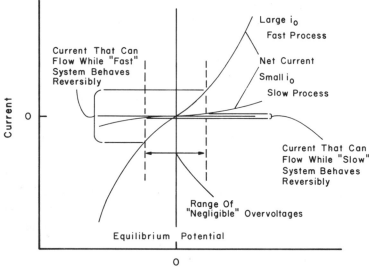

When $\eta = 0$, $i = i_0$, so that

$$i = i_0 \exp[-\alpha n F \eta / RT]$$

and

$$\eta = (RT/\alpha n F) \ln i_0 - (RT/\alpha n F) \ln i \qquad (2\text{-}16)$$

which is the Tafel equation (2-1) introduced earlier.

Thus, the present kinetic treatment is compatible with the experience accumulated with irreversible processes as well as with the accepted description of equilibrium situations.

18

A general equation connecting net current flow, i, and potential can then be written as follows:

$$i = i_f - i_b \qquad (2\text{-}17)$$

Using equations (2-4) to (2-7), and (2-12),

$$i = nFAk\{C_o \exp[-\alpha nFE/RT] - C_R \exp[1-\alpha)nFE/RT] \qquad (2\text{-}18)$$

When applying this equation in practice, it is important to recall that C_o and C_R are concentrations *at the surface,* or *effective* concentrations; these are not necessarily (nor even usually) the same as the bulk-phase concentrations. A modification of this equation, taking into account differences in electrical potential between surface and bulk, is presented in Section 3.6.2.

2.2.3 Operational Definition of Reversibility

It was pointed out in Section 1.3 that electrochemical systems may behave reversibly or irreversibly depending on the experimental conditions. Here, it will be shown that a kinetic view of the charge-transfer process permits one to decide whether or not a particular system is likely to behave reversibly.

By definition, reversible behavior means that the Nernst equation (or a theory based on the assumption of Nernstian behavior) fits observed results. The degree of fit necessary is a function of the experiment. For instance, in potentiometric work, reversibility means that the actual electrode potential is indistinguishable from the equilibrium potential, and "indistinguishable" varies according to the accuracy with which differences in potential can be observed — in some experiments small fractions of a millivolt may be significant whereas in other cases a few millivolts may be negligible. The concept of the exchange current enables one to discuss this question in quantitative terms.

Figure 2-2 demonstrates that the overvoltage increases (though not linearly) as the net current increases. For a given overvoltage, a larger net current will flow if the exchange current is greater — the slope of the curve of net current *vs.* overvoltage increases with the magnitude of the exchange current (for not too large overvoltages). In other words, since a particular magnitude of overvoltage is "negligible" in a given series of experiments, systems with large exchange-currents ("fast" systems) are less likely to behave irreversibly under current flow than are systems with small exchange-currents ("slow" systems): more current can be drawn from the fast system before the "appreciable" overvoltage is reached.

This argument can be made quantitative on the basis of the equations derived in Section 2.2.2. At equilibrium (zero net current),

$$i_o = i_f = i_b$$

$$= nFAkC_o \exp[-\alpha nFE_{eqm}/RT] \qquad (2\text{-}19)$$

$$= nFAkC_R \exp[(1-\alpha)nFE_{eqm}/RT] \qquad (2\text{-}20)$$

where E_{eqm} emphasizes that the equilibrium potential is being considered.

Equation (2-18) refers to conditions where net current flows, and the potential in that equation is a non-equilibrium potential, E_{neq}:

$$i = nFAk\{C_o \exp[-\alpha nFE_{neq}/RT] - C_R \exp[(1-\alpha)nFE_{neq}/RT]\} \qquad (2\text{-}21)$$

Dividing the three terms in equation (2-21) by i_o, by equation (2-19), and by equation (2-20) respectively,

$$i/i_o = \exp[-\alpha nF\eta/RT] - \exp[(1-\alpha)nF\eta/RT] \qquad (2\text{-}22)$$

where $\eta = E_{neq} - E_{eqm}$, by definition of the overvoltage η.

Thus, the relationship between net current flow, overvoltage, and exchange current can be readily calculated. Some illustrative values are given in Table 2-1. It is seen, for instance, that if the overvoltage is not to exceed 0.1 mV, then the net current must not be more than 0.39% of the exchange current (if n=1); however, if overvoltages of 10mV can be tolerated, then the net current may be as high as ca. 30-50% of the exchange current (again for n=1, the exact amount depending on the value of α).

Table 2-1   Ratio (i/i_o), of net current to exchange current for different overvoltages

η		$n = 1$		(i/i_o)	$n = 2$	
	$\alpha = 0.2$	0.5	0.8	0.2	0.5	0.8
0.1 mV	0.00390	0.00390	0.00391	0.00780	0.00782	0.00783
1 mV	0.0386	0.0390	0.0395	0.0763	0.0782	0.0800
10 mV	0.350	0.392	0.442	0.634	0.802	1.01
100 mV	2.14	6.89	22.3	4.76	49.9	517

This discussion of reversibility pertains only to the charge-transfer step itself; it provides an insight into the relationship between observed reversibility and the current flowing, in the absence of complications arising as a result of other reaction-steps. These considerations are applicable fairly directly to potentiometric work: stable and reproducible potentials are set up, and are measurable, only if the system has a sufficiently large exchange-current, but this need not be large since the current drawn in potentiometric measurements is very small indeed.

In other situations, the relative rates of the charge-transfer step and of the other steps determine whether or not reversibility is observed. In polarography, for instance, a reversible polarographic step results if the charge-transfer process is sufficiently fast relative to diffusion, for then the current, limited by the rate of diffusion, is not sufficiently large as to disturb the Nernstian behavior of the electroactive species at the electrode. Irreversibility can result if charge transfer is not fast relative to diffusion, or to chemical or other coupled reactions.

Reference electrodes are half-cells whose potential does not change under the experimental conditions used. Frequently, experimentation involves the flow of current. Too large a current will produce changes of the potential, and therefore useful reference electrodes employ electrochemical systems with large exchange-currents. Equation (2-14) shows that one can also improve a given reference-electrode system if the area of the reference electrode is made larger, since the exchange current is directly proportional to the area of the electrode. In some modern instruments, the circuit is arranged so that negligible current flows through the reference electrode; though it is not the primary purpose of such circuits, this makes the choice of reference electrode less critical (see Section 7.4.2 on three-electrode circuits).

2.2.4 Inadequacies of the Theory

One inadequacy of the theory as presented became evident in Section 2.2.1: the equations are written without a precise definition of the process to be described, other than that it involves charge transfer. This presentation is not unique to the discussion given here, but is representative of treatments currently available in the literature (see, however, Section 2.2.5).

One can distinguish several types of electrode processes involving charge transfer in somewhat different ways: redox changes at an inert electrode (e.g., Fe(II)/Fe(III) at mercury); reactant and product soluble in different phases (e.g. Cd(II)/Cd(Hg)); electrodeposition (e.g. Cu(II)/Cu). In the first case, the charge-transfer process is an electron-transfer process from electrode to solution or *vice versa*; in the second case, electrons may neutralize the cadmium(II) ion with subsequent transfer of the cadmium atom into the amalgam phase, or the ion may be incorporated into the electron cloud of the mercury and discharged "simultaneously" with, or "after", transfer of the ion; in the third case, it is likely that the ion is transferred to the electrode material before (or simultaneously with) charge neutralization.

In various processes, changes in complexation (including solvation) and effects of crystal-lattice forces may also be important. There is no *a priori* reason why one type of energetic and kinetic description should fit these various reactions, yet that is what is implicitly postulated in the present treatment. These assumptions are all embodied in the idea that the electrode potential can be apportioned into two parts, the fraction (αE) assisting reduction and the remainder hindering the oxidation (in the German literature, (αE) is regarded as assisting the oxidation). Hence, the question of the validity of the theory requires a discussion of the physical significance of the transfer coefficient α and the implicitly assumed constancy of α with changing electrode potential.

The historical development of the concept of the transfer coefficient, and of the physical significance associated with it by various workers, has been discussed in detail in a recent review (7). For the present purpose, therefore, the most important ideas only will be mentioned.

The definition of the transfer coefficient according to equations (2-6) and (2-7) carries an implication that α is independent of potential. In point of fact, no theoretical reason why this should be so has been put forward (but see Section 2.2.5), and there exists insufficient experimental evidence to support or to contradict this assumption.

If the charge-transfer step is visualized in terms of the intersection of Morse curves referring to reactant and product, the transfer coefficient results as the ratio of the slopes of the curves at the intersection. This is illustrated in Figure 2-3, which follows the classical paper of Horiuti and Polanyi (8) on the reduction of hydrogen ions.

The application of a potential is regarded as raising the Morse curve of the charged species (H^+ or H_3O^+), while the curve for the reduced, uncharged, species is unaffected. Thus, the height of the energy barrier (measured from the point of intersection of the Morse curves for reactant and product) is changed by a fraction (α) of the applied potential (E). If the shape of the Morse curve is unaltered (though it is shifted upward), and if the curves are approximately linear near the point of intersection, then α — which depends on the ratio of the slopes at the intersection — will be independent of E.

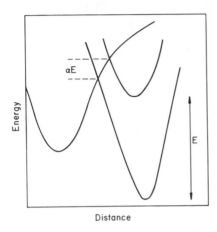

Fig. 2-3 Reduction process according to Horiuti and Polanyi (8). The electrode potential affects the energy of the hydrogen ion but not of the reduced form. The change in activation energy is a fraction of the electrical energy and depends on the slopes of the curves in the region where they intersect (reproduced by permission).

Alternatively, one can postulate that the curve of energy *vs*. reaction-coordinate for the process is altered *progressively* by the application of a potential. For instance, the influence of the potential can be related to the distance of the reacting species from the surface, and α becomes a measure of the position of the activated complex in the electrical field at the interface (Figure 2-4).

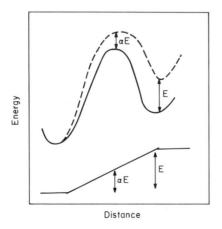

Fig. 2-4 Energy curve for reduction (after Christov (9), by permission of Bunsengesellschaft

Such views, and others, have been espoused by various people; they are not always mutually exclusive, and are usually plausible. However, they remain descriptions and not explanations in the absence of an explicit physical model of the charge-transfer process. On the other hand, some clearly wrong explanations of the transfer coefficient have been offered; for details and further discussion of the question as a whole, the literature (7) should be consulted.

Another unsatisfactory feature of the theory is the assumption that n electrons may be transferable in a single stage which can be described in the same way as a single-electron transfer. This question has barely been raised, let along discussed.

In summary, the treatment outlined is empirically useful. It provides a description that is compatible with the broad outline of experience with irreversible and with reversible processes. Kinetic parameters (k, α, i_0) are used, determination of which has been a goal that has spurred much effort, and a great deal of understanding has been gained in the process. However, there is no satisfactory model to sustain the theory, in particular the implied constancy of α with potential.

2.2.5 Modern Theories of Charge Transfer

The idea that charge transfer at electrodes involves a change of activation energy brought about by variation of the electrode potential lies at the heart of the theory discussed in the preceding sections. However, other factors are ignored, for example the influence of the potential on the energy states of the reacting species and the energy changes resulting from solvent reorientation around the reacting species. The influence of the potential on the energy levels of the reaction species ("double-layer effect") is nowadays taken into account by a modification of the expressions for the effective potential and for the concentrations of the reactants at the electrode (see Section 3.6.2), but this is done *ad hoc* rather than as an integral part of the consideration of all the factors that determine the activation energy of the charge-transfer step. Some comparatively recent work, however, has started from a detailed consideration of all these factors, and the salient features of this work will be indicated below.

There are two groups of theoretical treatments involved. In reactions such as the liberation of hydrogen, the formation and breaking of chemical bonds is involved, and the treatments (10) include some necessarily arbitrary assumptions as to the influence of the electrode potential on the bond-forming process. Moreover, these treatments are inevitably specific to the reaction considered, and no general conclusions result as to, for instance, the question of what physical significance there might be in the concept of the transfer coefficient.

Another group of reactions is that involving transfer of electrons only. Here, there are accompanying changes in the coordination shell surrounding the reacting ions and in the orientation of solvent molecules around them. The energies associated with such changes can be calculated using, for example, theories of dielectric media — theories of some generality, so that results could give insight into this whole class of reactions. Details of these studies have been discussed in recent reviews and articles (11), and an excellent qualitative introduction is available (12). The treatments have been applied both to heterogeneous electron-transfer at electrodes and to homogeneous electron-transfer between ions in solution. The salient result for electrode processes is that the free energy of activation, ΔG^*, is given (12) by the expression

$$\Delta G^* = \frac{W_1 + W_2}{2} + \frac{\lambda}{8} - \frac{\eta en}{2} + \frac{1}{2\lambda} (\eta en + W_1 - W_2)^2 \tag{2-23}$$

where W_1, W_2 are the energies involved in bringing the reacting species from the bulk phase to the electrode surface; e is the electronic charge; and λ is given by

$$\lambda = n^2 e^2 \left\{ \frac{1}{a} - \frac{1}{r} \right\} \left\{ \frac{1}{D_{op}} - \frac{1}{D_S} \right\} \tag{2-24}$$

with a the ionic radius (including coordination shell); r is twice the distance between the electrode and the center of the ion; D_{op} is the square of the refractive index of the solvent; and D_S is the static dielectric constant.

The electrode potential influences ΔG^* not only directly by the presence of the overvoltage η but also through the electrostatic parts of the work terms W_1 and W_2 (i.e., the double-layer effect described in Section 3.6.2 is explicitly considered). Equation (2-23) shows that, in general, ΔG^* is a quadratic function of η, whereas equations (2-6) and (2-7) embody the assumption that ΔG^* is a linear function of η. Alternatively, one can say that if equation (2-23) is applicable, then the transfer coefficient of equations (2-6) and (2-7) will itself be a function of the electrode potential.

However, if the work terms W_1 and W_2 are negligibly small, and the overvoltage is also small, (2-23) becomes

$$\Delta G^* \doteq \frac{\lambda}{8} - \frac{\eta en}{2} \tag{2-25}$$

so that the transfer coefficient becomes independent of potential, and equal to 1/2.

Experimental support for this theory comes from various studies on electron transfer in homogeneous reactions, and from comparison of data between homogeneous and electrode processes for similar systems. Details and references can be found in the previously mentioned reviews (11). As far as the transfer coefficient is concerned, i.e., whether it is independent of potential or whether some potential dependence can be found as predicted by equation (2-23), the question remains open. One study (13) reported a potential dependence in good agreement with equation (2-23), but later work on the same system (14) did not support this conclusion.

2.3 Determination of Kinetic Parameters

The thermodynamic theory of electrochemical reactions provides a basis for analyzing processes in terms of the chemical species present in the bulk phase(s) and of the overall energetics involved. As usual, this type of analysis cannot provide an insight into the mechanisms or rates of the reactions (except of course that under equilibrium conditions one can identify the species whose presence in the bulk phase affects the electrode potential).

Analysis of kinetics provides a means for identifying which reaction steps in the overall process are rate-determining, and the rates of these steps can be found. The rates of electrochemical processes are frequently limited by steps other than the charge-transfer itself, and therefore electrochemical measurements provide an avenue for the determination of the rates of various processes: for instance, polarography permits the determination of diffusion coefficients of electroactive species under conditions (plateau of the polarographic step) where diffusion is the rate-determining step; the rates of various chemical reactions have also been studied when these are rate-determining. The procedure is straightforward when a single step in the overall process is rate-determining; however, when two or more steps are of comparable rate and these steps are conjointly rate-determining, calculation of the rates of the individual steps rests on an analysis based on a model for the interrelation between these steps, and usually one varies experimental conditions so that the relative rates of these slow steps change somewhat: for instance, variation of frequency in a.c. polarography affects the diffusion and charge-transfer steps to different extents and often permits determination of the rate constants for both processes.

Frequently, mathematical analysis of the models is difficult, and limited progress has been made in the study of reactions with mixed control by two or more steps, in comparison with the understanding gained of reactions with but a single rate-limiting step.

The kinetics of the charge-transfer step itself has naturally been of the greatest interest to electrochemists. The above generalizations apply, in that determination of rates is easier and more reliable when the charge-transfer step is the only rate-limiting one; other situations have yielded to analysis in a number of instances, but much remains to be done. Here, some remarks on the significance of the kinetic parameters of the charge transfer will be made.

The exchange current, or preferably the exchange-current density, is a measure of the inherent rate of the charge transfer; as indicated in Section 2.2.3, the observation of reversible or irreversible behavior can be rationalized in terms of the amount of current that is (or is not) negligible in comparison to the exchange current. Equation (2-14) shows that the exchange current depends on the concentrations of the electroactive species; thus, i_0 is not the same at all equilibrium potentials and knowledge of the magnitude of i_0 under one set of experimental conditions does not necessarily permit calculation of i_0 for other situations. A more complete characterization of a processs is possible if the exchange current is determined at two potentials, at each of which C_0 and C_R are known: then k and α can be calculated. With knowledge of k and α, the exchange current can be calculated for any (other) values of C_O and C_R.

The significance of α has been discussed in Section 2.2.4. Use of this parameter in the way described above presupposes that its magnitude does not vary appreciably with potential, and this may not be the case (Section 2.2.5). Furthermore, it is thereby assumed that α does not depend on the concentrations of the electroactive species; in one theory of charge-transfer, however, a dependence on concentration is implied (15).

The standard rate-constant k can be obtained from i_0 values as described above, or directly if analysis of the experiment is performed in the appropriate way. In any case, equation (2-14) incorporates information on the units of the rate constant: setting $C_O = C_R = C$ for convenience, it is clear that

$$kC = i_0/nFA \qquad [\text{amp/coulomb. mole}^{-1}\text{ cm}^2] \qquad (2\text{-}26)$$

If C has the units mole/cm^3, then k has units of cm.sec.$^{-1}$; this differs from the units for the rate constant of a homogeneous process by the presence of the unit of length. The rate of a heterogeneous process depends on the rate at which reactive species enter the reaction layer at the surface, and this depends on the thickness of this layer: units of length thus must appear in the rate constant, when rates are written in terms of concentration per unit volume.

The same conclusion can be reached, perhaps in a more familiar way, by writing the concentration not as a volume, but as a surface concentration, mole/cm^2: then k would have the units of sec.$^{-1}$, which is comparable with the units for a first-order rate-constant of a homogeneous reaction (except that the latter also includes cm^3 mole^{-1}, since the total amount of reaction increases in proportion to the reaction volume; with homogeneous reactions, the habit has been to work in terms of the total amount of reaction, whereas with heterogeneous processes one generally works in terms of amount per unit area). The use of surface concentration again embodies the concept of a reaction layer at the surface: surface concentration here means the concentration *effectively at the surface,* i.e. within "striking" distance. This poses a problem and presents an area of uncertainty: methods for measuring or calculating surface concentrations must either involve assumptions about the thickness of a reaction layer, or about the equivalence of thermodynamically and kinetically significant magnitudes (see Section 3.3 for a discussion of this point).

Thus, interpretation of the significance of values of k must rest on a model that takes into account the heterogeneous character of the charge-transfer step and that explicitly considers the movement in space that is corollary to the transfer of charge.

For reversible processes, the formal standard potential is taken as the reference potential and the value of k obtained refers to that potential. There is no ambiguity involved since the result does not depend, for instance, on the nature of the reference half-cell used in the experiment. For irreversible processes, however, the values of k obtained are *relative to the potential scale chosen:*

From equation (2-15), we have for irreversible processes

$$\eta = (RT/\alpha nF) \ln (nFAkC_O) - (RT/\alpha nF) \ln i \qquad (2\text{-}27)$$

The rate constant k can be obtained by extrapolation of the linear part of the curve η-vs.-(ln i) to $\eta = 0$: k is obtained from the extrapolated value for i together with the known values of n, F, A, C_O. However, for irreversible processes the equilibrium potential is usually not known and therefore the absolute magnitude of the overvoltage is also not known. Experiments are carried out, for instance, in obtaining Tafel plots (Figure 2-1), by measuring current as a function of the voltage applied between the working electrode and some reference electrode. The extrapolation is then made to *zero applied voltage* and values of k are calculated on this basis and reported in units of cm.sec.$^{-1}$. These values then depend on the reference half-cell used, since the criterion of zero applied voltage depends on this. Therefore, it should be remembered that reported values of rate constants for irreversible reactions depend on the reference electrode (or potential) chosen. This is not the case for reversible processes, or processes for which the standard potential is known, since the values of k there refer explicitly to a known half-cell potential on the hydrogen-electrode (or some other) scale, that potential being determined by the system itself and not by a calculation in which an arbitrary or conventional potential scale is used.

Therefore, one cannot obtain *absolute,* only *relative,* rate constants for irreversible processes. Corollary to this, one could obtain absolute rate constants for irreversible processes only if the absolute *electrical* single-electrode potential of the reference half-cell were known; the impossibility of obtaining this information has been pointed out in Section 1.2.1.

Conversely, if the absolute value of a heterogeneous charge-transfer rate-constant were known, an absolute electrical single-electrode potential could be calculated. Such a procedure has indeed been suggested (16); however, that suggestion has the following weaknesses:

a) In considering the dependence of rate constant on potential, as in equations (2-6) or (2-7), a standard state of zero absolute electrical potential is implied if the potential, E, is not referred to a reference half-cell. No such standard state is experimentally achievable since no absolute values for electrical potentials of half-cells exist.

b) In the calculations, the distance factor of heterogeneous rate-constants (see above) is ignored. The matter may appear to have been taken into account by the use of surface rather than of volume concentrations, but this is not sufficient in the absence of a discussion as to how the *effective* surface-concentratration might be measured or calculated (see Section 3.3).

In summary, two matters should be kept in mind concerning published values for the kinetic parameters of charge-transfer processes at electrodes (much of this available data has been compiled and classified by type of system (17)). Firstly, the experimental difficulties are considerable, more so for faster processes where conditions under which charge transfer is the sole limiting processes are difficult to achieve; in the analysis of the results, further uncertainties accrue because of the need to correct for non-faradaic currents, possible double-layer effects (Section 3.6), adsorption processes (Section 5.4 and 5.5), and so on. Secondly, and related to this problem of the analysis of experimental data, existing physical models for the charge-transfer process remain largely hypothetical and somewhat speculative.

2.4 References

1. L. Gierst and H. Hurwitz, *Z. Elektrochem.*, *64* (1960) 36
2. H. Shirai, *Nippon Kagaku Zasshi, 82* (1961) 339; *Chem. Abstr. 55:*14127h
3. F. von Sturm and M. Ressel,*Microchem. J., 5*(1961) 53
4. S.I.Woodburn, T.J. Cardwell and R.J. Magee, *Rec. Trav. Chim. Pays-Bas, 88*(1969) 1167
5. F.M.Hawkridge and H.H.Bauer, *Anal. Chem., 44* (1972) 364
6. J.Newman, *J. Electrochem. Soc., 113* (1966) 1235; and references given there.
7. H.H.Bauer, *J. Electroanal. Chem., 16* (1968) 419; see also J. Brenet, *Electrochim. Acta, 13* (1968) 457; M. Bonnemay, G. Bronoel and M. Savy, *Electrochim. Acta, 13* (1968) 659
8. J. Horiuti and M. Polanyi, *Acta Physicochim. URSS, 2* (1935) 505
9. S.G.Christov, *Z. Elektrochem., 62* (1958) 567
10. For example: M. Salomon, C.G.Enke and B.E. Conway, *J. Chem. Phys., 43* (1965) 3989
11. R.A.Marcus, *Ann. Rev. Phys. Chem., 15* (1964) 155; V.G.Levich, *Adv. Electrochemistry Electrochemical Engng., 4* (1966) 249; X. de Hemptinne, *Bull. Soc. Chim. Belg., 77* (1968) 21.
12. R.A.Marcus, *Trans. Symposium Electrode Processes, Philadelphia 1959* (Wiley 1961), p. 239
13. R. Parsons and E. Passeron, *J. Electroanal. Chem., 12* (1966) 524
14. F.C.Anson, N.Rathjen and R.D.Frisbee, *J. Electrochem. Soc., 117* (1970) 477
15. H. Gerischer, *Z. Physik. Chem., 26* (1960) 223, 325
16. M. Salomon, *J. Electrochem. Soc., 113* (1966) 940
17. N. Tanaka and R. Tamamushi, *Electrochim. Acta, 9* (1964) 963

CHAPTER 3

The Electrical Double-Layer

3.1 Definition

When a metal is in contact with an electrolyte, electronic charge on the metal attracts ions of opposite charge-sign to the interface. There exists then a layer of charge in the metal and a layer in the electrolyte — hence the term "electrical double-layer".

Actually the situation is more complicated. The potential within the electrolyte does not change discontinuously, but over a distance near the surface, as a result of a finite distance of approach of the ions and of thermal agitation. Even in the metal, the potential is not uniform up to the surface, since the electron "cloud" is not completely spatially coincident with the lattice of metal ions. Therefore, there is a separation of charge at the surface of a metal, somewhat akin to a double layer. (This dipolar effect is one of the points that must be considered in any discussion of single-electrode potentials: the effect will inevitably vary in magnitude according to the nature of the phase that is in contact with the metal — i.e., the *electrical* dipole-effect varies according to the *chemical* interactions involved. This is the reason why measurements of work functions in vacuum cannot be used for calculations of dipole effects at the metal-electrolyte interface).

The dipolar effect at a metal surface is usually neglected in discussions of electrode processes. The distances involved are certainly much smaller than those in the electrolyte, where the change of potential with distance is appreciable over several atomic diameters at the least. However, some important work is being done at semiconductor-electrolyte interfaces (1), where a double-layer structure in the semiconductor has considerable influence. Here, we will restrict our discussions to metal-electrolyte systems and consider the double layer to reach only into the solution phase: i.e., we consider the electrical potential in the metal to be uniform from the bulk metal up to the metal-electrolyte boundary; in the solution, the electrical potential varies from the surface to the bulk phase.

It turns out that more is involved than the presence of two layers of charge, as will become evident below. Nevertheless, the term "electrical double-layer" has continued in use, and describes that whole region around the interface in which the potential changes from its bulk value in one phase to its bulk value in the other phase.

3.2 Electrocapillarity

"Electrocapillarity" describes those phenomena at interfaces that concern the relation between surface tension and electrical charge. These phenomena have long been studied, and there exist thermodynamic relations that enable us to interpret the

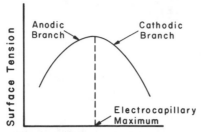

Fig. 3-1 Electrocapillary curve (schematic).

interfacial tension between a metal and the solution of an electrolyte in terms of the structure of the double layer. Mercury is the only conveniently available liquid metal at room temperature, making it an obvious choice for measurements of surface tension, and our present quantitative understanding of the electrical double-layer rests almost exclusively on the interpretation of work carried out with mercury electrodes (although a little work has been done, e.g., with liquid gallium, Woods metal, lead at elevated temperatures).

Measurements of the interfacial tension between mercury and aqueous salt solutions show that the interfacial tension depends on the potential of the mercury (with respect to some reference electrode) and also on the nature of the salt. The relationship between tension and potential is of an approximately parabolic nature (see Fig. 3-1).

This relationship can be qualitatively understood as the result of two effects: the inherent surface-tension of the mercury, and electrostatic repulsion in the plane of the surface. A net charge on the metal attracts ions of the opposite charge to the surface and to a first approximation we can visualize two layers of charge of opposite sign at the surface, one layer inside the electrode and the other on the solution side. The charges of like sign tend to repel one another along the plane of the interface, i.e. there is a tendency for the surface to spread out, or in other words the net surface-tension is decreased by the presence of the charge. This will be the case whether the net charge on the metal is positive or negative.

We can then infer that the maximum interfacial tension corresponds to the situation where there is zero net charge on the metal. The applied potential at which this situation is reached is called the *electrocapillary maximum* (e.c.m.) or the *potential of zero charge* (p.z.c.); commonly used symbols are E_{ecm} and E_{pzc}.

Graphs (e.g. Fig. 3-1) showing the relationship between surface tension and potential are called electrocapillary curves. The portion of the curve at potentials where the metal carries a negative charge (i.e. potentials negative to the potential of zero charge) is termed the cathodic branch of the electrocapillary curves and that at more positive potentials is called the anodic branch.

It is important to realize that the potential of zero charge does not correspond to a

30

situation in which an "electrostatic potential" inside the electrode is equal to that in the bulk of the solution (i.e. to an "absolute" electrical potential difference of zero between metal and electrolyte): forces other than these electrostatic ones may be present in the system and may manifest themselves in differences of potential across the interface. For instance, it is very likely that the molecules of water are not oriented in a random fashion at the interface between mercury and aqueous solution, and if there is a predominant orientation of the water molecules, the resultant dipole-moment will produce a difference of potential across the interface even in the absence of a net charge on the metal.

If the nature of the electrocapillary curves were determined only by the potential (or charge) applied to the metal and by the properties of the solvent, then with a given reference electrode the shape of the electrocapillary curve, and the potential of zero charge, would be independent of the nature of the salt. It turns out that this is not the case: the nature of the curves is very markedly influenced by the nature of the electrolyte (see Fig. 3-2).

In solutions of the alkali halides, the anodic branch of the electrocapillary curves shows decreased interfacial tension in the sequence chloride→bromide→iodide. The potential of zero charge correspondingly moves to more negative potentials, and the magnitude of the interfacial tension at the potential of zero charge decreases progressively. This type of behavior can be qualitatively explained by invoking the idea of *specific adsorption of anions.*

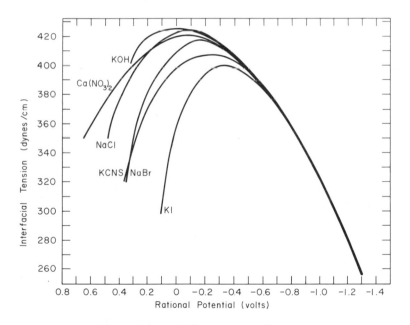

Fig. 3-2. Interfacial tension of mercury in contact with aqueous solutions of the salts named; T = 18°C. Abscissas are measured relative to a "rational" scale in which the potential difference between the mercury and a capillary-inactive electrolyte is arbitrarily set equal to zero at the electrocapillary maximum (after Grahame (2), by permission of American Chemical Society).

Specific adsorption describes the situation in which an ion is present at the surface in greater amount than required by electrostatic forces. Then, there will exist a net charge on the solution side of the interface even in the absence of electrostatic charge imposed on the metal from an external polarizing source. The presence of this charge decreases the interfacial tension (in the way discussed earlier). In the example considered here, the interfacial tension is progressively lowered on the anodic branch of the electrocapillary curves, that is at potentials where the electrode carries a positive charge and the solution side of the electrical double-layer is composed predominantly of anions. Consequently, these observations can be explained on the basis that halide ions are specifically adsorbed to an increasing extent in the order chloride→bromide→ iodide.

The electrocapillary maximum corresponds to zero net charge in the double layer. With specific adsorption of anions, this situation can be attained only when sufficient cations are brought into the double layer to neutralize the charge due to specifically adsorbed anions. In order to reach this point, a more cathodic potential must be applied to the electrode than in the absence of specifically adsorbed anions. Thus, the point of zero charge moves to more cathodic potentials with specific adsorption of anions, as in Fig. 3-2. With specific adsorption of cations, the shift would be to anodic potentials.

The quantitative study of phenomena such as this has permitted us to obtain a reasonably good understanding of the main features of the electrical double-layer. On the whole, it turns out that anions are very commonly specifically adsorbed to some extent, whereas inorganic cations are less commonly specifically adsorbed to an appreciable extent. Also, evidence for the specific adsorption of fluoride ions is rather doubtful, and it has been quite common practice to take the electrocapillary behavior of sodium or potassium fluoride solutions as a reference system in which specific adsorption of both cations and anions is presumed absent.

It is possible that these differences among the various inorganic ions result to a great extent from the fact that cations are commonly hydrated in aqueous solution, whereas anions (with the exception of fluoride) seem to be hydrated to a very much smaller extent. On this hypothesis, the hydrated cations can approach the interface to an extent that is limited by the presence around the cation of the hydration shell, and the possibility of short-range interaction between the cation and the electrode material does not arise; thus, the hydrated species interacts with the electrode only as a result of electrostatic forces, which is by definition characteristic of *non*-specifically adsorbed species. Anions, without an hydration shell, can approach the surface much more closely and some type of short-range interaction can occur, perhaps the formation of incipient covalent bonds.

These ideas lead to a model of the electrical double-layer in which one distinguishes two layers of closest approach of ions to the surface; anions can approach more closely than can cations. The plane of the electrical centers of specifically adsorbed anions is termed the *inner Helmholtz plane*, these ions forming the *inner Helmholtz layer.* Non-specifically adsorbed ions do not approach as closely, they are present in the *outer Helmholtz layer,* and the plane through the electrical centers of these ions forms the *outer Helmholtz plane*. These layers together form the *compact* or *rigid double-layer*. However, the presence of a net charge on the electrode does not result merely in the formation of a compact layer of ions whose charge balances completely the charge present in the metal; on the solution side of the compact layer, there is a region in which ions of one sign predominate over ions of the other, and moving further away from the electrode the concentrations of charges of opposite sign become progressively more nearly equal, until the situation of electroneutrality that exists in the bulk of the solution is reached. The region between the compact layer and the bulk of the solution is termed the *diffuse double-layer*.

Quantitative understanding of the double-layer structure is based on two types of experiments and theories. On purely thermodynamic grounds, it is possible to derive relationships between interfacial tension and the excesses of anions and cations present at the interface; however, these theories do not lead to a model such as that described above, and it is necessary to introduce non-thermodynamic reasoning in order to relate the total surface-excesses to quantities that apply to the various regions within the compact and diffuse layers. We shall now briefly review the thermodynamic and non-thermodynamic theories commonly in use.

3.3 Thermodynamic Treatment

A number of complete and rigorous treatments of this subject are available (2,3). Here, once again, we shall discuss only the essential principles involved and attempt to avoid one of the sources of confusion that is often encountered.

In the treatment by Gibbs (4), which has been followed by later workers, quantities characterizing the interface between the two phases are derived by considering the two phases to be in contact. An interfacial tension (σ) results, and corollary discontinuities in the phases, from the dividing surface toward the bulk of each phase. This situation is compared with the hypothetical one where the composition of the phases is uniform right up to the dividing surface, within both phases. By subtraction, one obtains the quantities that describe the equilibrium energetics of the interface itself, and the most convenient expression for the present purpose is the Gibbs adsorption equation at constant pressure and volume, namely

$$(d\sigma)_{P,V} = -\Gamma_1 d\mu_1 - \Gamma_2 d\mu_2 - \dots \qquad (3\text{-}1)$$

where the Γ's are surface-excess concentrations in moles per unit area and the μ's are the chemical potentials of the corresponding species in the bulk phases.

It is to be noted that there is no restriction on the spatial distribution of the molecules making up the surface-excess concentrations; in particular, there is no justification in the theory for regarding these molecules as concentrated in a thin layer at the dividing surface itself; rather, one has to bear in mind the possibility that the surface-excess quantities have finite values at appreciable distances from the dividing surface. Thus, thermodynamically derived surface-concentrations may not be suitable values for the surface concentrations that are kinetically effective in a heterogeneous process, a problem that arises in relation to the significance of charge-transfer rate-constants (Section 2.2.4).

Based on equation (3-1), one frequently sees written equations such as

$$\left(\frac{\partial \sigma}{\partial \mu_1}\right)_{\mu_2, \ldots P, V} = -\Gamma_1 \tag{3-2}$$

which would indicate that the surface-excess concentration of component 1 can be obtained by measurement of the change of interfacial tension as a function of the chemical potential of species 1, keeping all other chemical potentials constant. The chemical potential is related to the activity, a, by an equation of the form

$$\mu = \mu_0 + RT \ln a \tag{3-3}$$

Frequently, one can simplify matters by neglecting activity coefficients and writing

$$\mu = \mu_0 + RT \ln C \tag{3-4}$$

where C represents concentration; then, equation (3-2) becomes

$$\frac{1}{RT}\left(\frac{\partial \sigma}{\partial (\ln C_1)}\right)_{\mu_2, \ldots, P, V} = -\Gamma_1 \tag{3-5}$$

This equation seems to show how surface-excess concentrations can be obtained experimentally, by measuring surface tension as a function of the concentration of the relevant species.

It is often said that surface concentrations derived in this way depend on the choice of position of the Gibbs dividing surface with respect to the actual interface between the phases. That seems reasonable, but on the other hand one wonders how it could come about that the experimental measurement of interfacial tension as a function of concentration could yield results that depend on the choice of a dividing surface in a theoretical model. This paradox is resolved, and the physical significance of the surface-excess concentration can be better visualized, by introducing into equation (3-1) the thermodynamic relationship between the various chemical potentials of all the species in any given system, namely, the Duhem relationship at constant pressure and volume,

$$n_1\, d\mu_1 + n_2\, d\mu_2 + \ldots = 0 \tag{3-6}$$

where the n's are the numbers of moles of the various species in the bulk phases.

We see that a change in the chemical potential of any one species can be expressed in terms of the changes in the chemical potentials of the other species, e.g.

$$d\mu_1 = -\frac{n_2}{n_1}\, d\mu_2 - \frac{n_3}{n_1}\, d\mu_3 - \ldots \tag{3-7}$$

This expression describes quantitatively the fact that one cannot, at constant pressure and volume, change the chemical potential of any one species while maintaining the chemical potentials of *all* the other species constant. In other words, the type of experiment suggested by equation (3-5) is impossible; if one changes the concentration of species 1 at constant pressure and volume, then the activity of at least one other species will thereby be altered. Substituting equation (3-7) into (3-1),

$$(d\sigma)_{P,V} = -d\mu_2 \left(\Gamma_2 - \frac{n_2}{n_1}\Gamma_1\right) - d\mu_3 \left(\Gamma_3 - \frac{n_3}{n_1}\Gamma_1\right) - \ldots \qquad (3\text{-}8\text{-})$$

and correspondingly

$$-\left(\frac{\partial\sigma}{\partial\mu_2}\right)_{P,V,\mu_3\ldots} = \Gamma_2 - \frac{n_2}{n_1}\Gamma_1 = \Gamma_{2(1)} \qquad (3\text{-}9)$$

This equation, and not equation (3-5), is one that can be applied directly to achievable experimental situations. One can vary the chemical potential of species 2, keeping constant the chemical potentials of species 3,4 . . . . and permitting the chemical potential of species 1 to change as required by equation (3-6). The rate of change of interfacial tension with change in chemical potential of species 2 then gives the surface-excess concentration of species 2 *relative to the surface-excess concentration of species 1;* this is frequently called the *relative surface-excess* of species 2 with respect to species 1.

Thus, experimental determination of surface-excess quantities involves the choice of one component of the system as a reference substance; the activity of that substance is not directly controlled, but varies as the activities of the other species are changed. Observed surface-excesses of these other species are then magnitudes relative to the surface excess of the reference substance. In the terminology of dividing surfaces, this procedure is equivalent to one in which the Gibbs dividing surface is chosen so as to make the surface excess of the reference substance zero. The statement that surface excesses depend on the choice of a dividing surface means that surface excesses depend on the choice of a reference component in the system.

Equation (3-9) shows that if the absolute surface-excesses, Γ_1 and Γ_2, are in the same ratio as these species exist in the bulk (i.e., if $\Gamma_1/\Gamma_2 = n_1/n_2$), then the surface tension will not change when the amount of species 2 is changed — because by varying the activity of species 2, the activity of species 1 is automatically changed by a corresponding amount. On the other hand, if Γ_1/Γ_2 is not equal to n_1/n_2 — the usual case — then $\left(\Gamma_2 - \frac{n_2}{n_1}\Gamma_1\right)$ has a finite magnitude, and represents the relative surface-excess of species 2 with reference to species 1; the interfacial tension changes as the amount of species 2 is varied. The reference species (in this case, species 1) is chosen in practice by permitting the activity of that species to change as required by the Duhem relationship (equations (3-6) and (3-7)) while the activities of all the other species are controlled: usually, varying one and keeping the remainder constant as in equation (3-9).

For the type of situation that concerns us, that of a solution containing a number of different components, it is generally convenient to make the solvent the reference substance. Then, if one is dealing with dilute solutions, $n_1 \gg n_2$ and the relative surface-excess $\left(\Gamma_{2(1)}\right)$ of species 2 is a good approximation to the absolute surface-excess concentration (Γ_2) *provided that the solvent itself does not have too high a surface concentration* (i.e. if Γ_1 is not too large). This assumption is very frequently made, but it is to be noted that it remains an assumption, and there is no reason why this assumption should always be a valid one; nor is there a way of experimentally checking the validity of this assumption. It is also worth recalling that $\Gamma_{2(1)}$

35

and Γ_2 refer to the whole discontinuity around the interface, and not to any defined distance from the surface. The assumption that all the molecules comprising $\Gamma_{2(1)}$ or Γ_2 are concentrated in a monomolecular layer at the surface has no foundation in the theory, and must rest in each case on some independent evidence about the particular system.

So far, this treatment has not specified the type of interface considered and is directly applicable only to uncharged species and phases. However, it has been shown (2,3) that the treatment can be applied also to the interface between an electrode and a solution of charged species by introducing the additional variable q, the *surface-charge density* on the electrode. The Gibbs equation then becomes

$$(d\sigma)_{P,V} = -qdE - \Sigma\Gamma_i d\mu_i \qquad (3\text{-}10)$$

A question arises as to the physical significance of the electrical potential, E, in this equation. For the moment, we can take this to be the potential applied to the electrode of interest with respect to a reference electrode whose potential does not change during the experiments; and we assume that liquid-junction potentials are absent or constant. Then, at constant composition we have

$$\left(\frac{\partial\sigma}{\partial E}\right)_{\mu_i} = -q \qquad (3\text{-}11)$$

which is the so-called Lippmann equation. This important result shows that the slope of the electrocapillary curve at any point is the charge density on the surface.

In the case of an ideally polarized electrode, the electrical behavior of the interface can be described in terms of the behavior of an electrical capacitor. Neglecting the possibly complicated structure of the double layer on the solution side of the interface, one can consider the system as analogous to a parallel-plate capacitor. The electrode carries a charge density q, and an equal charge of opposite sign, -q, is present in the solution; consequently, we can define the *static* or *integral capacity*, K, of the electrical double-layer as

$$K = q/E \qquad (3\text{-}12)$$

The potential difference in this equation should be the potential difference between the two plates of the equivalent electrical capacitor. However, the "absolute" difference of electrical potential across the electrical double-layer is not an accessible quantity. Therefore, the capacity K defined in this way is *conventional* and not absolute, and its magnitude depends upon the choice of a reference scale for the potential difference.

Furthermore, the capacity of the electrical double-layer is not independent of potential, differing in this respect from the capacity of conventional capacitors. It is therefore convenient to define the *differential capacity*, C, by the relationship

$$C = \frac{dq}{dE} \qquad (3\text{-}13)$$

This formulation takes into account the fact that the capacity is a function of potential. C is a quantity that can be determined experimentally in absolute terms since it does not depend on the choice of a reference potential. The determination of C can be carried out directly by several electrical methods (see Section 7.3) or by double differentiation of electrocapillary curves since, from equations (3-11) and (3-13),

$$C = \frac{\partial^2 \sigma}{\partial E^2} \qquad (3\text{-}14)$$

The relationship between C and K can be seen by equating the surface charge-density from the two expressions (3-12) and (3-13):

$$\frac{\partial q}{\partial E} = C = K + E \frac{\partial K}{\partial E} \qquad (3\text{-}15)$$

When E is zero, the differential capacity equals the integral capacity. Most commonly, the reference potential chosen in this connection is the potential of zero charge; a potential scale with the potential of zero charge set by convention to be zero is termed the *rational scale of potential*. This scale (and the corollary equality of C and K at the electrocapillary maximum) is widely used in calculations concerned with the structure of the electrical double-layer.

The experimental situation normally considered is one in which the reference electrode maintains a fixed potential. This has the disadvantage that, when the composition of the solution of interest is changed, the liquid-junction potential between the test solution and the solution in the reference half-cell changes. An alternative possibility is to use a reference electrode that is reversible to one of the ions of the test solution, and to allow the reference electrode to assume different equilibrium potentials according to the concentration of the solution; for instance, in studying chloride solutions of varying concentration, one might use a calomel reference electrode — a 0.1M calomel electrode if the test solution is 0.1M chloride, a 1M calomel electrode when the test solution is 1M in chloride, and so on. Then the change (dE in equation (3-10)) of potential of the indicator electrode is equal to the change (dE⁻ or dE⁺, see below) in the potential applied from the external circuit together with the change (dE) of the potential of the reference half-cell due to the changing composition of the electrolyte. In this situation, the adsorption equation for charged species becomes

$$(d\sigma)_{P,V} = -q dE^- - q dE' - \Gamma_+ d\mu_+ - \Gamma_- d\mu_- \qquad (3\text{-}16)$$

where E⁻ refers to a potential applied between the indicator electrode and a reference electrode that is reversible to the anion of the test solution (E⁺ would denote a scale based on a reference electrode reversible to the cation) and subscripts +, - refer to cations and anions respectively.

The reference-electrode potential E, by definition of reversibility (Nernstian behavior) with respect to anions, follows the relation

$$d\mu_- = z_- F dE \qquad (3\text{-}17)$$

where z_- is the charge on the anion, including magnitude and sign (similarly, z_+ for the cation). If the formula of the salt considered is $M_{v_+}N_{v_-}$, where v_+, v_- are the number of cations and anions respectively per salt "molecule" then

$$v_+ z_+ = -v_- z_- \qquad (3\text{-}18)$$

Further, $\qquad\qquad\qquad d\mu = v_+d\mu_+ + v_-d\mu_-$ (3-19)

The surface-charge density, q, on the electrode is equal in magnitude but opposite in sign to the charge density in the solution part of the double layer, so that

$$q = -(z_+F\Gamma_+ + z_-F\Gamma_-)$$ (3-20)

Combining equations (3-16) to (3-20) yields

$$(d\sigma)_{P,V} = -qdE^- - (\Gamma_+/v_+)d\mu$$ (3-21)

Similarly, for a reference electrode reversible to cations, one can obtain

$$(d\sigma)_{P,V} = -qdE^+ - (\Gamma_-/v_-)d\mu$$ (3-22)

and from these last two equations,

$$-v_+\left(\frac{d\sigma}{d\mu}\right)E^- = \Gamma_+$$ (3-23)

$$-v_-\left(\frac{d\sigma}{d\mu}\right)E^+ = \Gamma_-$$ (3-24)

Thus, by maintaining constant the potential applied from the external circuit (E^- or E^+), and measuring the change of interfacial tension with changing chemical potential of the *salt*, the relative surface-excesses of cations and of anions can be obtained separately: in the first case by using a reference electrode that is reversible to the anion of the electrolyte, in the second by using a reference electrode that is reversible to the cation. These important results open the way to the investigation of the roles of cations and anions individually in determining the structure of the electrical double-layer.

In the special case where the charge on the electrode is zero, equations (3-21) and (3-22) yield

$$(d\sigma)_{P,V} = -(\Gamma_-/v_-)\, d\mu = -(\Gamma_+/v_+)\, d\mu$$ (3-25)

and $\qquad\left[\left(\dfrac{d\sigma}{d\mu}\right)_{P,V}\right]_{ecm} = -\Gamma_-/v_- = -\Gamma_+/v_+ = -\Gamma_{salt}$ (3-26)

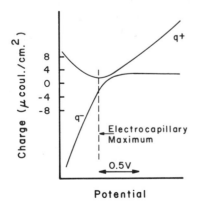

Fig. 3-3. Surface-excess charges due to cations (q^+) and anions (q^-) in the double layer; 0.3M NaCl, 25°C (after Grahame (2), by permission of American Chemical Society).

i.e., the change of surface tension with chemical potential of the salt yields the surface excess of the salt at the potential of zero charge.

Fig. 3-3 shows the type of results obtained by application of these equations to the solution of an electrolyte. We may note the following points:

a) At the point of zero charge, the sum of the charges due to the surface excesses of anions and cations is zero, in accord with the definition of the point of zero charge.

b) The charge attributable to a surface excess of *anions* will be *negative* when this surface excess is a positive quantity, e.g. at anodic potentials. Fig. 3-3 shows that, at sufficiently cathodic potentials, the charge due to anions is positive, i.e. the *surface excess of anions is negative.* In other words, the surface-excess charge of positive sign in the double layer at a negatively charged electrode can be attributed in part to cations attracted to the surface (positive surface-excess of cations) and in part to anions repelled from the surface (negative surface-excess of anions) — there are more cations present than if the surface were uncharged, and fewer anions.

c) The surface excess of cations is positive at both cathodic and at anodic potentials. This contrasts with the behavior of the anion in this system. Such observations are typical for most salts, and are explicable on the assumption that the anion is specifically adsorbed:

At the potential of zero charge, there is an appreciable surface-excess of the salt; this arises as a result of some inherent surface-activity of the anions or of the cations, not from electrostatic considerations. On the anodic branch (positively charged electrode), the surface excess of cations increases; from electrostatic considerations, the opposite would be expected. Therefore, the surface excess of cations must result from attraction by anions in the double layer. For excess cations to be attracted, the charge due to excess anions must be greater than the positive charge on the electrode i.e., the anions must be specifically adsorbed.

It is sometimes said that specific adsorption indicates the presence of a specific interaction between the adsorbed species and the electrode itself. This may be so, for instance, in the case of halide ions at mercury — but specific adorption may occur also because the species is "sqeezed out" from the aqueous environment, as is commonly the case with organic species but probably also with, for instance, nitrate ion. Thus, the occurrence of specific adsorption cannot be automatically taken to indicate the presence of particular adsorptive forces between the electrode and the specifically adsorbed species.

3.4 Theory of the Diffuse Double-Layer

3.4.1 Assumptions

Thermodynamic theory can lead to information about total surface-excess quantities, but not about the spatial distribution of the relevant species within the double layer. Electrostatic theory provides a plausible framework for describing the structure of the diffuse double-layer, which is sufficiently far from the electrode that short-range interactions with the electrode are not important. This electrostatic theory is discussed here.

It is assumed that within the diffuse double-layer, the relationship between the potential and the distribution of charge is (as in any electrostatic field) described by the Poisson equation which, for the one-dimensional case, is

$$\frac{d^2\phi}{dx^2} = -4\pi\rho/D \tag{3-27}$$

where ϕ is the potential, x the distance coordinate, ρ the electrical charge per unit volume, and D the dielectric constant of the medium.

Furthermore, it is assumed that the distribution of energies of the ions follows the Boltzmann relation

$$n_i^d = n_i^B \exp\left(-w_i^d/k_B T\right) \tag{3-28}$$

where n_i^B is the total number of ions per unit volume in the bulk of the solution, k_B the Boltzmann constant, and n_i^d the number of ions in a region of the double layer where work w_i^d is expended in bringing an ion from the bulk of the solution. The work is given by

$$w_i^d = z_i e\phi \tag{3-29}$$

where e is the electronic charge and z_i the valency of the ion.

Application of these equations involves the assumptions that

a) The dielectric constant does not vary with distance from the electrode, see equation (3-27).

b) The work involved in bringing an ion from the bulk of the solution is purely electrostatic — i.e., displacement of other species is not considered, nor is any rearrangement of the hydration sheath of the incoming ion, nor the finite volume of the latter.

c) The system has no structure (i.e., the dielectric is a continuum).

d) There are no specific effects such as ion-pairing.

Results of this theory have been quite successful in elucidating double-layer structure and the effect of the latter on the faradaic behavior of redox systems. Thus, the above assumptions are good ones, better perhaps than one would expect; this matter has been recently discussed in detail by Mohilner (3). It appears that the worst defect of the simple theory is the lack of recognition given to the fact that the outer

40

Helmholtz plane may be situated at different distances from the surface for different ionic species.

Here, only the most important results of the simple theory will be presented; the derivations, starting with equations (3-27) to (3-29), can be found in several reviews and books (2,3,5).

3.4.2 Charge in the Diffuse Layer

The charge density, q^d, in the diffuse double-layer is given by

$$q^d = \int_{x_0}^{\infty} \rho dx \tag{3-30}$$

where x_0 is the coordinate of the outer Helmholtz plane. By use of equations (3-27) to (3-29), and integrating, one obtains

$$q^d = (\pm) \left\{ (Dk_BT/2\pi) \; \Sigma n_i^B \; (\exp\left[- z_i e_0 \phi^{\circ}/k_BT\right]-1) \right\}^{1/2} \tag{3-31}$$

where ϕ° is the "potential at the outer Helmholtz plane" — i.e., the difference of potential between this plane and the bulk of the solution. For a z-z-valent salt, $z_+ = z_- = z$ and $n_+^B = n_-^B = n^B$, so that equation (3-31) becomes

$$q^d = (2k_BTn^BD/\pi)^{1/2} \; \sinh \; (ze_0\phi^{\circ}/2k_BT) \tag{3-32}$$

or, at 25°C, approximately

$$q^d \doteq 11.7 \; C^{1/2} \sinh \; (19.52 \; z\phi^{\circ})$$

where concentration, C, replaces number of ions per unit volume, n^B.

The applicability of these equations can best be judged by comparing observed values of differential capacity with estimated ones. The potential difference between metal and solution, ϕ_m-ϕ_s, is composed of potential differences across the compact layer, ϕ_m-ϕ°, and across the diffuse layer, ϕ°-ϕ_s:

$$\phi_m\text{-}\phi_s = (\phi_m\text{-}\phi^{\circ}) + (\phi^{\circ}\text{-}\phi_s) \tag{3-34}$$

Then,
$$\frac{\partial}{\partial q_m} \; (\phi_m\text{-}\phi_s) = \frac{\partial}{\partial q_m} \; (\phi_m\text{-}\phi^{\circ}) + \frac{\partial}{\partial q_m} \; (\phi^{\circ}\text{-}\phi_s) \tag{3-35}$$

where q_m is the charge on the metal (in absence of specific adsorption, $q_m = -q^d$). Equation (3-35) can be written in terms of the differential capacities of the whole double-layer (C), of the compact double-layer (C^i) and of the diffuse double-layer (C^d):

$$\frac{1}{C} = \frac{1}{C^i} + \frac{1}{C^d} \tag{3-36}$$

This equation forms the basis for one check of the validity of the theory outlined above (sometimes called the Gouy-Chapman[-Stern] theory): certain assumptions are made about C^i; C^d is calculated using the derivative of equation (3-31) or of equation (3-32):

$$C^d = \frac{\partial q^d}{\partial \phi^{\circ}} = ze_0 \; (n^BD/2\pi k_BT)^{1/2} \; \cosh \; (ze_0\phi^{\circ}/2k_BT) \tag{3-37}$$

41

and then C, calculated from equation (3-36), is compared with experimental values of C.

The assumption that C^i is a constant leads to curves of capacity vs. potential that are symmetrical about the point of zero charge, a situation not found in practice. However, the assumption that C^i has a constant value anodic to the p.z.c., and another but also constant value at cathodic polarizations, produces curves that are similar to experimental ones (Fig. 3-4).

Grahame calculated C^i as a function of charge for 1M sodium fluoride from measurements of C and calculation of C^d from the theory outlined above. Then, he calculated values of C for other concentrations of sodium fluoride on the assumption that C^d varied (equation (3-37)) while C^i remained constant at a given value of q^d. The results were in encouraging agreement with experimental values of C (Fig. 3-5).

Of interest is a possible dependence on frequency (of the measuring signal) of the differential capacity. If the capacity is invariant with frequency, then the processes involved in charging the double layer occur essentially instantaneously; a variation with frequency, on the other hand, would indicate that there is a time lag. Such a time lag could result from movement of the ions involved and/or reorientation of solvent (water) molecules. It is generally agreed (7) that reorientation of water molecules would not lead to an observable time-lag at the frequencies normally used (< 100 kHz), though suggestions have been made (8) that such an effect might be observed, especially at solid electrodes.

The effect of movement of the ions has been considered (9), and it seems that a variation of capacity with frequency may result at frequencies above ca. 3 MHz in solutions more dilute than ca. 10^{-2} M. It is possible that the phenomenon could be used to investigate double-layer structure in solutions that are dilute and have high resistance.

3.4.3 Components of Charge in the Diffuse Layer

The charge in the diffuse double-layer due to the presence of cations (q_+^d) and that due to the presence of anions (q_-^d) can be calculated from equation (3-30) in a similar way to that used for obtaining the total charge q^d. Instead of equation (3-32), one then has

$$q_+^d = (k_B T n^B D/2\pi)^{1/2} [\exp(-ze_0\phi^\circ/2k_BT)-1] \qquad (3\text{-}38)$$

and
$$q_-^d = -(k_B T n^B D/2\pi)^{1/2} [\exp(ze_0\phi^\circ/2k_BT)-1] \qquad (3\text{-}39)$$

These equations can be compared with experimental results for systems where specific adsorption is absent, using the identities

$$q_+^d = zF\Gamma_+^d \qquad (3\text{-}40)$$

$$q_-^d = -zF\Gamma_-^d \qquad (3\text{-}41)$$

42

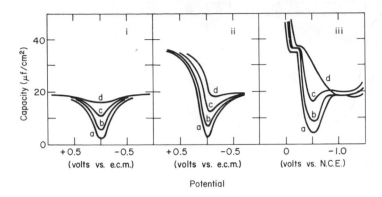

Fig. 3-4. Double-layer capacities at various concentrations – a: 10^{-4}M; b: 10^{-3}M; c: 10^{-2}M; d: 10^{-1}M for i: constant C^i (20 μf/cm^2); ii: C^i = 20 μf/cm^2 at negatively charged electrode, C^i = 38 μf/cm^2 at positively charged electrode; iii: experimental results for chloride solutions. Figure from Parsons (6), by permission of Butterworths.

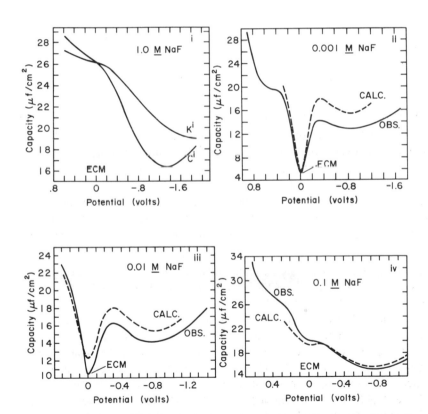

Fig. 3-5. Double-layer capacity for sodium-fluoride solutions – i: calculated from experimental data; ii, iii, iv: experimental (OBS) and calculated (CALC) using inner-layer capacity from i and diffuse-layer capacity from theory. From Grahame (2), by permission of American Chemical Society.

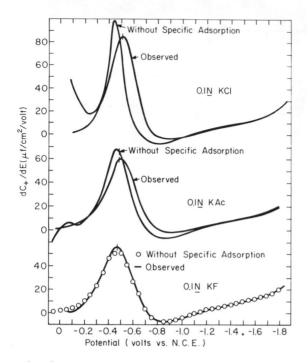

Fig. 3-6. Observed and calculated values of dC_+/dE; calculated values assume the absence of specific adsorption (after Grahame and Soderberg (10), by permission of American Institute of Physics).

Γ_+^d, Γ_-^d can be taken as approximating the experimentally obtainable quantities Γ_+ and Γ_- (equations (3-23) and (3-24); it will be recalled that these are relative surface-excess, the reference substance normally being water).

Such comparisons with experiment were made by Grahame and Soderberg (10). For convenience, the comparisons were in terms of (dC_+^d/dE) rather than q_+^d, where

$$C_+^d = \left(\frac{\partial q_+^d}{\partial E}\right)_\mu \tag{3-42}$$

Fig. 3-6 shows the very good fit between theory and experiment for 0.1M potassium fluoride, and discrepancies found with acetate and with chloride solutions, in accord with the view that fluoride is not specifically adsorbed, whereas acetate and chloride are.

It is worth noting that at increasingly cathodic polarization ($\phi^\circ \rightarrow -\infty$), while q_+^d of course increases monotonically, q_-^d reaches a finite, *positive,* limiting value (see equations (3-38) and (3-39)). This reflects the repulsion of anions from the negatively charged surface, shown in Fig. 3-3 and discussed in connection with that figure. Similarly, at increasingly anodic polarization one would reach a situation where the charge due to cations is negative; however, this is not found in practice since systems so far investigated have shown specific adsorption of anions at sufficiently anodic potentials (there is no firm agreement to date as to the possible specific adsorption of fluoride ion at highly anodic potentials). The theoretical limiting values of charge due to repelled anions (or cations) are, from equations (3-38) and (3-39),

$$\left| \begin{array}{c} \text{limit} \\ \\ \phi^\circ \to \pm\infty \end{array} \left(q_{\mp}^d \right) \right| = (k_B T n^B D / 2\pi^{1/2} \qquad (3\text{-}43)$$

At 25°C this is approximately 5.9 $C^{1/2}\mu$coul./cm², in good agreement with the value of ca. 3μcoul./cm² for 0.3M sodium chloride, Fig. 3-3.

3.4.4 Potential Distribution in the Diffuse Layer

The integrated form of equation (3-27) can be combined with an equation similar to (3-31) to obtain the variation of potential with distance from the electrode in the form

$$\phi = \pm(4k_B T/ze_0)\tanh^{-1}(\exp[-Kx^1]) \qquad (3\text{-}44)$$

Since this equation applies only to the diffuse layer, it is useful to take x^1 as the distance from the outer Helmholtz plane; then, the left-hand-side of the equation represents potential with respect to ϕ°, the potential at the outer Helmholtz plane. In this equation

$$K = 2ze_0(2\pi n^B/Dk_B T)^{1/2} \qquad (3\text{-}45)$$

$$\doteq 3.3. \times 10^7 zC^{1/2} \ cm^{-1} \quad (\text{at } 25°C) \qquad (3\text{-}46)$$

At sufficiently large values of Kx^1, equation (3-44) becomes

$$\phi \doteq \pm(4k_B T/ze_0)\exp[-Kx^1] \qquad (3\text{-}47)$$

so that the potential varies exponentially with distance from the electrode. The "half-thickness" of the diffuse double-layer is then

$$\text{Half-thickness} = (\ln 2)/K \quad (\text{definition})$$

$$\doteq 2.1 \times 10^{-8}/zC^{1/2} \ cm. \quad (\text{at } 25°C) \qquad (3\text{-}48)$$

In solutions of molar strength, this is of the order of magnitude of the ionic radius of unsolvated ions; thus, the diffuse double-layer if of rather limited extent in moderately concentrated solutions. Instead of half-thickness, one could calculate the thickness of the diffuse layer within which any prescribed portion of the whole potential drop occurs; Table 3-1 gives values for the thickness of the region within which 99.99% of the diffuse-layer perturbation occurs.

The potential gradient in the diffuse double-layer, $d\phi/dx$, is obtained in the same type of derivation: at 25°C in aqueous solution,

$$\frac{d\phi}{dx} \doteq 0.15 \times 10^6 \ q^d \ \text{volts/cm.} \qquad (3\text{-}49)$$

where q^d is in μcoul./cm². The charge density in the diffuse layer is generally no higher than 20μcoul./cm², so that the field strength has a maximum value of ca. 3×10^6 volts/cm.

45

Table 3-1. Thickness of the Diffuse Double-Layer (in which 99.99% of the whole potential drop across the layer occurs); from Mohilner (3) (by permission of Marcel Dekker)

Electrolyte* Concentration	Ionic Charge	Thickness of Layer (99.99% of diffuse-layer effect)
10^{-6} M	1	28 000 A$^{\circ}$
	2	14 000
	3	9 400
10^{-4}	1	2 800
	2	1 400
	3	940
10^{-2}	1	280
	2	140
	3	94
10^{-1}	1	88
	2	44
	3	30

*z-z-valent electrolyte considered

3.4.5 Potential at the Outer Helmholtz Plane

The potential at the outer Helmholtz plane can be calculated if q^d is known — see equations (3-31) and (3-32). In the absence of specific adsorption, the total charge in the double layer is equal to the charge in the diffuse double-layer; then, q^d can be obtained from electrocapillary data (see equation (3-11)) or from measurements of differential capacity (and then integrating: see equation (3-13)). Thus, it is a quite straightforward matter to obtain values of ϕ° for systems in which specific adsorption is absent. The dependence of ϕ° on potential and on concentration is shown in Fig. 3-7 for solutions of sodium fluoride. In systems where the anion is specifically adsorbed, the values in Fig. 3-7 will still be approximately correct at cathodic polarization; the stronger the adsorption of anions, the more cathodic the potential at which the ϕ° values become similar to those in Fig. 3-7.

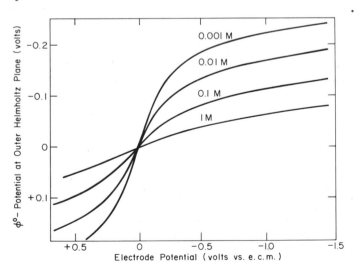

Fig. 3-7. Potential of the outer Helmholtz plane as a function of the rational potential for the Hg|NaF(aq.) electrode at 25°C (after Parsons (11), by permission of John Wiley).

46

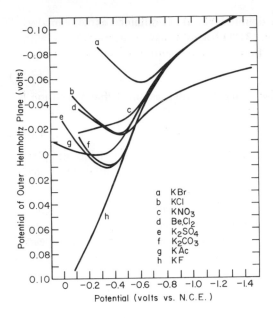

Fig. 3-8. Potential at the outer Helmholtz plane; tenth-normal aqueous solutions at 25°C (after Grahame and Soderberg (10), by permission of American Institute of Physics).

For systems where specific adsorption of anions is appreciable, the potential at the outer Helmholtz plane is obtained by a less direct approach. First, Γ_+ values are obtained by measuring surface tension as a function of salt concentration and applying equation (3-23) (or from capacity measurements and a similar equation: see Grahame and Soderberg (10)). Then, equations (3-40) and (3-38) are used to calculate ϕ°. The assumption made in this calculation is that cations are not specifically adsorbed and that Γ_+ is therefore the cationic charge Γ_+^d present in the diffuse double-layer. The assumption that cations are not specifically adsorbed has stood the test of experience remarkably well; however, some exceptions are now known to the validity of this assumption (see Section 3.5).

Fig. 3-8 shows some values of ϕ° obtained in the way just described. It is apparent that specific adsorption of anions causes ϕ° to be more negative (i.e. approach of cations is spontaneous) at anodic polarizations; this correlates with the positive values of Γ_+ found at these potentials in such systems — cf. Fig. 3-3.

3.5   The Inner Double-Layer

The diffuse layer can be rather satisfactorily understood in terms of simple theory, as outlined in Section 3.4. The inner layer, on the other hand, has not yielded to simple theoretical approaches; present understanding comes almost entirely from experiment. The data is obtained for the whole double-layer by experiment, and the contribution of the diffuse layer substracted by means of the theory described above.

The charge due to adsorbed anions in the inner layer, q_-^i, for instance, is given by

$$q_-^i = q_- - q_-^d \qquad (3\text{-}50)$$

The total charge due to anions in the double layer, q_-, is obtained experimentally by the procedure indicated in equation (3-24) (or by capacity measurements, with the same reference electrode, as a function of salt concentration) and then using

$$q_- = -zF\Gamma_- \tag{3-51}$$

A similar procedure leads to knowledge of q_+. It is then assumed that the cation is not specifically adsorbed, so that

$$\Gamma_+ = \Gamma_+^d \tag{3-52}$$

Then, equations (3-40) and (3-38) yield the potential at the outer Helmholtz plane, ϕ°; the latter, in equation (3-39), then gives q_-^d. Thereupon, q_-^i is obtained by invoking equation (3-50).

Fig. 3-9 shows values of q_-^i calculated for the same conditions as Fig. 3-3, where only the values for the double-layer as a whole were given. It is seen that q_-^i is zero at sufficiently cathodic polarizations — specific adsorption of the anion disappears at an electrode carrying a sufficiently high negative charge. The charge due to anions in the diffuse double-layer, q_-^d, is seen to be positive at all potentials (i.e., Γ_-^d is negative). At cathodic polarizations, this results from the negative charge on the electrode, whereby anions are repelled from the interface; at anodic polarizations, the charge q_-^i is greater than the charge q_m on the electrode so that once again an anion in the diffuse layer "sees" net negative charge in the inner layer and is repelled.

Fig. 3-10 shows the amount of specifically adsorbed anions as a function of potential for various species. These data provide a comparison of the specific adsorbabilities of different anions; however, explanation of these differences in terms of the nature of the species is not a straightforward matter. For instance, one cannot assume that specific adsorption is in all cases a result of the same type of force: with halide ions, there probably is specific interaction with the (mercury) surface and even perhaps covalent bonding; on the other hand, adsorption of the nitrate ion is favored because this ion does not fit so well into the structure of the liquid water and tends to be "squeezed out". Thus, the fact that the amount of specifically adsorbed anions changes with potential to different degrees for different anions is not surprising.

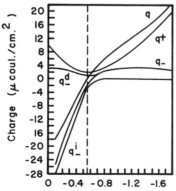

Potential (E⁻, volts vs. Calomel Electrode)

Fig. 3-9. Charge due to cations and anions in inner and diffuse layers; 0.3M NaCl, 25°C (after Grahame (2), by permission of American Chemical Society).

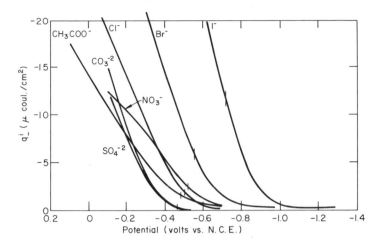

Fig. 3-10. Amount of specifically adsorbed anions for various electrolytes (0.1 normal) in contact with mercury at 25°C; vertical lines indicate point of zero charge (after Delahay (5), by permission of John Wiley).

It is generally agreed that specific adsorption implies that the species involved is not hydrated, at least not in the direction of the electrode; and that if covalent bonding is present, then specific adsorption is also. At the present time, however, one cannot predict whether a particular species will or will not be specifically adsorbed, and indeed one cannot even rationalize the behavior of the various species in a satisfactory manner. According to Devanathan and Tilak (12), specific adsorption increases with size of the ion, and they give the sequences F^-, $H_2PO_4^-$ $<OH^-$ $<Cl^-$, NO_3^- , ClO_4^- , IO_3^- , BrO_3^- $<Br^-$ $<SCN^-$ $<I^-$; Li^+ $<Na^+$ $<K^+$ $<Rb^+$ $<Cs^+$ $<Tl^+$; and $(CH_3)_4N^+$ $<(C_2H_5)_4N^+<(C_3H_7)_4N^+$.

The specific adsorption of the anions is considerably more pronounced than that of the cations. Indeed, for many years it was thought that inorganic cations were not adsorbed; now, however, strong evidence is available (13) for the specific adsorption of at least some cations at mercury electrodes (Tl^+, Pb^{++}, Cs^+) and at platinum (Tl^+, Pb^{++}, Cd^{++}, Zn^{++}). The method for obtaining the amount of specifically adsorbed anions, described earlier in this section, was based on the assumption that the cation present is not specifically adsorbed. For situations where this is not a permissible assumption, other procedures must be followed. The principle, however, remains the same: electrocapillary (or capacity) data yield values for the *total* surface-excess (in compact and diffuse layers) and the amounts present in the diffuse layer, obtained by calculation, are subtracted from the total amounts to yield data for the specifically adsorbed portion. Details of this procedure can be found in the literature (14).

Reports of specific adsorption of inorganic cations indicate that this phenomenon is correlated with the presence of specifically adsorbed and/or complexing anions. It may well be, therefore, that such cations are adsorbed as ion pairs or complex species. On the other hand, larger organic cations such as the tetraalkyl ammonium

49

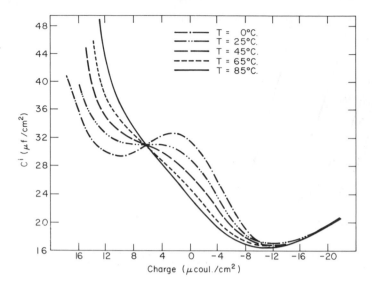

Fig. 3-11. Calculated capacity C^i of the compact double-layer for mercury in 0.8M sodium fluoride at several temperatures (after Grahame (15), by permission of American Chemical Society).

ions appear to be adsorbed "inherently", i.e. in absence of specifically active anions. The question of cation adsorption is referred to also in Sections 3.6.1 and 5.5.3.

The capacity of the inner layer can be calculated by equation (3-36) using experimental values of the total differential capacity and theoretically based values of the capacity of the diffuse layer, the latter obtained from equation (3-37) and experimentally obtained values for ϕ°. The differential capacity of the inner layer then appears to be strongly dependent on charge and temperature even in the absence of specific adorption (Fig. 3-11).

Similar calculations for different electrolytes indicate that the capacity of the inner layer is comparatively little affected by specific adsorption (see Fig. 3-12). However, this conclusion runs counter to intuitive expectation, and an alternative theory (12) begins with the assumption that the capacity in absence of specific adsorption has a fixed value irrespective of the charge of the electrode.

The capacity-*vs.*-potential plots frequently show a "hump" — e.g. Fig. 3-4(iii); Fig. 3-11 (low temperatures). This phenomenon has to be explained in terms of

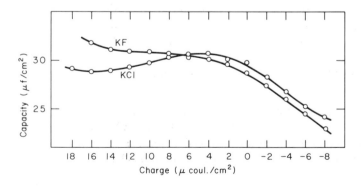

Fig. 3-12. Integral capacity of the compact double-layer for potassium chloride and for potassium fluoride (after Grahame and Parsons (16), by permission of American Chemical Society).

properties of the inner layer, but there is no agreement as to how this may be done. Some workers stress the role of water dipoles and picture the hump as due to re-orientation of the water molecules. However, this cannot be the whole story, since the humps depend on the nature of the electrolyte as well as of the solvent. For many electrolytes, the potential at which the hump appears corresponds (12) to an inflection on the plot of q^i *vs.* q_m, indicating the influence of adsorbed anions on this phenomenon.

Isotherms for specific adsorption, the related potentials ϕ^i at the inner Helmholtz plane, and other features of the inner layer are not yet well understood. Dielectric saturation, effects due to the discreteness of the charges, electrostriction, amongst other "physical" effects appear to be of importance. The original literature must be consulted for information about the changing, contemporary, theories of the inner layer. An authoritative recent review is that of Barlow (17).

3.6 Double-Layer Influence on Faradaic Processes

3.6.1 Introductory

The electrical double-layer is the environment in which reduction and oxidation pro-cesses occur. In many systems, the behavior of depolarizers has been found to de-pend on the nature and concentration of the supporting electrolyte in ways that cannot be explained by chemical interactions such as complex formation in the bulk of the solution, and in these cases an explanation is sought in terms of the types of double layers set up by the supporting electrolytes.

Phenomena ascribed to double-layer effects include the variation of hydrogen over-voltage with the nature of other cations and of anions present in the system (18); anomalous dips in polarographic diffusion-currents (19) (see Fig. 3-13); and varia-tions of the charge-transfer rate-constants: for example, bismuth (and antimony and arsenic) ions are reduced reversibly (in a.c. polarography) in the presence of chloride, bromide, or iodide ions but not in the presence of perchlorate; the rate constant for reduction of zinc ions decreases as the concentration of sodium perchlorate in-creases, but the rate increases in the presence of sufficient amounts of iodide (or bromide or chloride) ions.

Some of these effects are thought to be chemically specific — e.g., it is thought

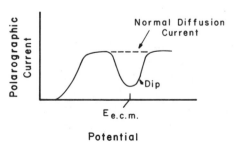

Fig. 3-13. Polarogram showing anomalous dip — usually near the potential of zero charge — observed in the reduction of a number of anions.

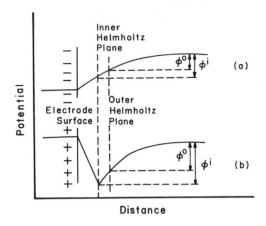

Fig. 3-14. Potential distribution in double layer: (a) no specific adsorption (in this case, at negatively charged electrode) (b) specifically adsorbed anions (here, at positively charged electrode).

that specifically adsorbed anions (Cl^-, Br^-, I^-) may act as "bridges" in the reduction of cations, the reducing electron being added while the cation is not directly at the electrode but held via the bridging anion. A number of recent papers have dealt with anion-induced adsorption of cations and the corollary effects on the charge transfer to the cation, including estimates of the stoichiometry (number of anions per cation) at the interface.

For instance, Pospisil and de Levie (20) correlated the surface excess of thiocyanate ion with the observed rate-constant for the reduction of In (III). It appears that the uncomplexed indium ion is the species present in the bulk of the solution, but that the rate-determining step at the interface involves two adsorbed thiocyanate ions for each In^{3+} ion; the reaction path is

$$In^{3+} + 2\ CNS^-(absorbed) \rightarrow In(CNS)_2^+(adsorbed)$$
$$In(CNS)_2^+ (adsorbed) + 3\ e^- \rightarrow In(Hg) + 2\ CNS^-(adsorbed)$$

Anson and Caja (21) found that the V(III)/V(II) reaction in presence of thiocyanate involves an adsorbed V(III)-thiocyanate complex containing one or more thiocyanate ions; the large exchange-current observed could be explained by the enhanced surface-concentration of reactant resulting from the adsorption.

Other cases of anion-induced adsorption of cations have been reported (e.g., for Cd(II), Zn(II), Pb(II) — see references 22-26). These observations on individual systems have not yet led to a general scheme or classification, and in the following we shall discuss in some detail only the general matter of how the potential distribution in the double layer is expected to influence the observed characteristics of the charge-transfer process.

The manner in which the potential varies with distance from the electrode depends on whether or not there is specific adsorption (potential distribution in the compact double-layer), and on the potential distribution in the diffuse layer (Section 3.4.4). This is shown schematically in Fig. 3-14. In the absence of specifically adsorbed ions, there is a continuous drop in potential from the surface into the bulk of the solution. However, when specific adsorption is present, the charge in the inner Helmholtz layer may be greater in magnitude than that on the electrode, since the ions present in the inner layer are held by adsorption forces in addition to electrostatic ones. Thus, the total charge on electrode plus inner layer may be negative, even when the charge on the electrode itself is positive.

Obviously, the approach of a charged depolarizer to the electrode is influenced by the sign and magnitude of the potential that is effective between the bulk of the solution and the region of the double layer where charge-transfer can occur. The potential may have an "equilibrium" effect — by making the concentration of the depolarizer at the surface different from the bulk value — or there may be a "dynamic" effect, where the rate of the overall process is influenced by the rate at which the charged species moves in the electrical field. These two effects — which are naturally limiting cases of the general one (27) — are discussed in the following sections.

3.6.2 Equilibrium Effects

An ion is in a different energy state in the double layer than in the bulk of the solution. Therefore, at equilibrium the concentration, C^{el}, of an ion that is about to take part in charge transfer at the electrode is related to the bulk concentration by

$$C^{el} = C^B \exp(-zF\phi^e/RT) \qquad (3\text{-}53)$$

where ϕ^e is the potential at the place of closest approach of the depolarizer to the electrode, with respect to the potential in the bulk of the solution. The potential effective in promoting charge transfer is that between the depolarizer at its closest approach, and that of the electrode. If the latter is E, relative to the solution, then the effective potential is $(E-\phi^e)$. Using this relationship and equation (3-53) together with the general equation for charge transfer derived earlier (equation (2-18)),

$$(i/nFAk) = C_o \exp[-z_o F\phi^e/RT]\exp[-\alpha nF(E-\phi^e)/RT]$$
$$-C_R \exp[-z_R F\phi^e/RT]\exp[(1-\alpha)nF(E-\phi^e)/RT] \qquad (3\text{-}54)$$

where z_o, z_R are the charges (with sign) on the oxidized and reduced species. Rearranging, and using

$$z_o - n = z_R \qquad (3\text{-}55)$$

yields

$$(i/nFAk) = \exp[(\alpha n - z_o)F\phi^e/RT]\left\{C_o\exp[-\alpha nFE/RT] - C_R\exp[(1-\alpha)nFE/RT]\right\} \qquad (3\text{-}56)$$

Therefore, if an experiment is analyzed by use of equation (2-18), the rate constant obtained there — the apparent rate-constant k_{app} — will be related to the rate constant calculated by equation (3-56), i.e. taking into account electrostatic effects, by

$$k_{app} = k \exp[(\alpha n - z_o)F\phi^e/RT] \qquad (3\text{-}57)$$

similarly, for the exchange current

$$(i_o)_{app} = i_o \exp[(\alpha n - z_o)F\phi^e/RT] \qquad (3\text{-}58)$$

Table 3-2. Calculated Apparent Rate-Constants and Potential at Outer Helmholtz Plane

Supporting Electrolyte	Thallium (I) k(corrected) = 2.00 assumed		Cadmium (II) k(corrected) = 0.04 assumed		Zinc (II) k(corrected) = 0.3 × 10^{-3} assumed	
	ϕ^e(mv)[a]	k_{app}(cm.sec^{-1})[b]	ϕ^e(mv)[c]	k_{app}(cm.sec^{-1})[d]	ϕ^e(mv)[e]	k_{app}(cm.sec^{-1})[f]
1 M NaF	2.49	1.80	-8.5[g]	0.068	-44.2[g]	3.30×10^{-3}
0.1 M "	6.79	1.65	-21[g]	0.15	-90.8[g]	4.20×10^{-2}
0.01 M "	13.4[g]	1.45	-41.3[g]	0.53	-144[g]	7.60×10^{-1}
1M KCl	-45[h]	4.53	-40[h]	0.49	-45[h]	3.50×10^{-3}
0.1 M "	-21[h]	2.85	-25[h]	0.19	-89[h]	3.80×10^{-2}
0.02M "	-23[h]	2.96	-47[h]	0.76	-126[h]	2.90×10^{-1}
0.1 M KBr	-71.7[i]	7.65	-62.2[i]	2.00	-89.0[i]	3.80×10^{-2}
0.1 M KNO$_3$	-24.7[i]	3.05	-30.2[i]	0.26	-88.3[i]	3.66×10^{-2}
0.1 M K$_2$SO$_4$	7.8[i]	1.62	-9.5[i]	0.072	-88.2[i]	3.63×10^{-2}

a, c, e. At potentials of -0.45, -0.55, -1.05 v. vs. S.C.E. respectively, taken to be the standard potentials for these systems: e.c.m. = -0.51 v. in NaF. It was assumed that $\phi^e = \phi^o_c$.

b. Taking k_{app} = 1.8 in 1M NaF, α=0.5; cf. Randles (28).
d. Taking k = 4 × 10^{-2}, α=0.2; cf. Gerischer (29), Berzins and Delahay (30).
f. Taking k_{app} = 3.3 × 10^{-3} in 1M NaF, α=0.3; cf. Sluyters (31).
g. Russell (32).
h. Grahame and Parsons (16).
i. Grahame and Soderberg (33).

The difference between the corrected and apparent rate-constants can be enormous. The effect is illustrated in Table 3-2 for several systems for which plausible values of k, α, and ϕ^e have been assumed.

The calculated values shown in Table 3-2 indicate the extent to which double-layer structure can influence the apparent rate-constant:

a) For an electrolyte where specific adsorption is absent or very small (NaF), the reduction of cations is affected in opposite ways at potentials anodic (Tl(I)) and cathodic (Cd(II)), Zn(II)) to the e.c.m. The magnitude of the effect is smallest near the e.c.m. (Tl(I)) and greater as the potential is increasingly different from the e.c.m. (Cd(II), then Zn(II)).

b) In the presence of specific adsorption (KCl), change of concentration of the supporting electrolyte may increase or decrease the apparent rate-constant: going from 0.02M KCl to 1M, one expects a decrease in k_{app} followed by an increase for reductions near the e.c.m. (Cd(II)), but a monotonic decrease for processes far removed from the e.c.m. (Zn(II)).

c) Different supporting electrolytes at the same concentration can give quite different values of k_{app}.

d) Small changes in ϕ^e can produce large changes in k_{app}: for Zn (II), k_{app} changes by ca. 15% when ϕ^e changes from 88.2 to 90.8 mv.; for Cd(II), k_{app} changes by ca. 8% when ϕ^e changes from 40 to 41.3 mv.

Since ϕ^e values can be obtained only after considerable calculation and on the basis of several assumptions from double-layer-capacity measurements, it may be fruitful to look for information about ϕ^e from observations of redox processes, effects on the latter often being appreciably greater than the variations of ϕ^c itself. In other words, it may be worthwhile to use the behavior of redox systems as a method for probing the potential distribution in the double layer.

The observed value, α_{app}, of the transfer coefficient is also influenced by the double-layer structure. This has been discussed by Parsons (11), and that work should be

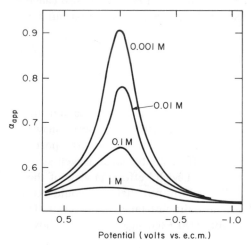

Fig. 3-15. Values of apparent transfer-coefficient – various concentrations of NaF: $\alpha = 0.5$, $z = +1$ (after Parsons (11), by permission of John Wiley).

55

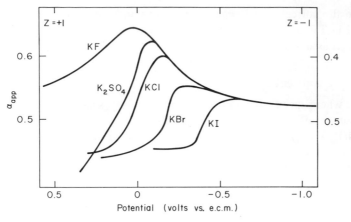

Fig. 3-16. Values of apparent transfer-coefficient for various electrolytes (0.1M): $\alpha = 0.5$, $z = \pm 1$ (left or right scales) (after Parsons (11), by permission of John Wiley).

consulted for details. Figs. 3-15 and 3-16 show variations of α_{app} expected, with a system where $\alpha=0.5$, for the cases where the concentration of a non-specifically adsorbed electrolyte is varied (Fig. 3-15) and for various electrolytes (Fig. 3-16).

Altogether, it is evident that double-layer effects are of profound importance in work where the kinetic parameters k and α are to be determined; and more generally in any studies where the kinetics of electrode processes are important. Present knowledge of double-layer effects is rudimentary: thus, there is evidence that in the presence of specific adsorption, the theory leading to equation (3-57) may be inadequate. One major uncertainty lies in the assignment of actual values to ϕ^e. At first, it may seem appropriate to use values of ϕ^0 since the latter is defined as the potential at the plane of closest approach of non-adsorbed ions, but that plane may be different for different species. Thus, setting $\phi^e = \phi^0$ for, say, the reduction of Zn^{++} in NaF means that one is assuming the same distance of closest approach to the electrode for $Zn^{++}_{(aq)}$ and for $Na^+_{(aq)}$ ions, an assumption that is almost certainly wrong. A great deal of further work on double-layer effects needs to be done.

The "equilibrium" double-layer effect described in this section is often also called the "static" or "Frumkin" effect (the fundamental idea involved was first put forward by Frumkin (34)).

3.6.3 Dynamic Effects

In cases where ϕ^e is large, and the electrostatic force between bulk phase and surface is appreciable, the rate of movement of a charged electroactive species may be influenced by the gradient of the electric field. Then, the rate of mass transport may be influenced by electrical migration in the diffuse double-layer as well as by diffusion. Such an effect is called a "dynamic" or "Levich" effect, in view of the work of Levich (35) on this problem. Generally, it turns out that one would expect to observe a dynamic double-layer effect only on quite fast faradaic processes. The expected relationship between measured and corrected exchange currents is shown

56

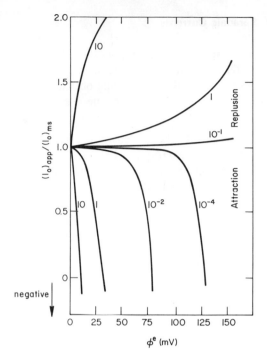

Fig. 3-17. Dynamic double-layer effect. Numerical values for uni-univalent electrolyte, millimolar depolarizer ($z_0 = 2$, $z_R = 0$): true exchange-current densities as shown, in amp./cm^2 (after Narayanan and Rangarajan (36), by permission of Commonwealth Scientific and Industrial Research Organization, Australia).

in Fig. 3-17, as a function of ϕ^e for systems with various inherent ("true", "actual") exchange currents. In this Figure, $i_{0(app)}$ represents the apparent exchange-current, which is related to the "true" or "inherent" value as described in equation (3-58), i.e. $i_{0(app)}$ reflects possible Frumkin-type double-layer effects; $(i_0)_{ms}$ is the measured value, i.e. obtained from the experimental data without applying corrections for any type of double-layer effect. The difference between these two quantities reflects the influence of electrical migration, i.e. a dynamic double-layer effect.

It is apparent from Fig. (3-17) that electrical migration has a significant effect only if ϕ^e and the "true" exchange-current are sufficiently large. It has been suggested that certain reported anomalous values of kinetic parameters could be explained by invoking this effect (11, 36).

It is interesting to note in Fig. 3-17 that, for a sufficiently large ϕ^e and attraction of the electroactive species, the observed exchange-current will become negative: as ϕ^e becomes larger for a given true exchange-current-density, the measured value, $(i_0)_{ms}$, of i_0 becomes increasingly larger until $(i_0)_{app}/(i_0)_{ms}$ becomes zero, i.e., $(i_0)_{ms} \to \infty$; for yet larger values of ϕ^e, the ratio is negative. Negative observed rate-constants have been reported and ascribed to this effect (37). Systems where such behavior exists can be used in "electrochemical oscillators" (38), which function analogously to electrical oscillators employing negative-resistance vacuum-tube or solid-state devices. The intriguing matter of negative rate-constants has recently been discussed also from a different point of view (39).

3.6.4 Separability of Faradaic and Non-Faradaic Currents

Until recently, it was universally assumed — implicitly if not explicitly — that one could always calculate the magnitude of a faradaic current by measuring the total current and subtracting the non-faradaic component, the latter being obtained in a separate experiment. However, Delahay (40) has suggested that this need not always be the case:

Consider a system M/M^+ at a potential E, and surface-charge density q corresponding to Γ_{M^+}. If the potential E is changed to $E+\Delta E$, $q \rightarrow q+\Delta q$ and $\Gamma \rightarrow \Gamma +\Delta \Gamma$. Now, the M^+ ions corresponding to $\Delta \Gamma$ can arrive in the double layer by two paths: from the solution, or by dissociation ($M \rightarrow M^+ + e^-$) at the interface. In the first case, "charging" (non-faradaic) current flows; in the latter, faradaic current. Since movement of ions from the solution takes a finite time, the current will be purely faradaic if the dissociation process is infinitely fast; on the other hand, if it is limitingly slow ("ideally polarized electrode") then the current is completely non-faradaic. Thus, the ratio of faradaic to non-faradaic in a given current depends on the time scale of the experiment; and one cannot equate the magnitude of either component with its value under other conditions.

The validity of this suggestion remains a matter of some controversy. In one type of situation, where an electrode at equilibrium is subject to a change of area, it does seem clear that the transient current that flows as the new equilibrium is established could be partly faradaic and partly non-faradaic according to the relative rates of the processes. However, where the disturbance from an initial equilibrium occurs by an imposed change of electrode potential, the supply of part of the charge in the double layer by the faradaic process could require the latter to proceed in the direction of reduction when the change of potential favors oxidation, an apparently unacceptable conclusion.

The most recent consensus of opinion appears to be that the question of *a priori* separability of faradaic and non-faradaic currents is of practical significance only for fast faradaic processes that involve specific adsorption of the electroactive species. The reader should consult the current and future literature for resolution of this problem. An excellent discussion of the publications in this area up to 1971 has been given by Smith (41); a wider-ranging review is that of Parsons (42).

3.7   References

1. H.Gerischer, *Physical Chemistry — An Advanced Treatise* (Academic Press 1970), *vol. IX A (Electrochemistry)*, ch. 5
2. D.C.Grahame, *Chem. Revs., 41* (1947) 441
3. D.M.Mohilner, *Electroanalytical Chemistry, 1* (1966) 241
4. J.Willard Gibbs, *The Collected Works, Vol.I* (Longmans Green 1931) pp. 219 ff.
5. P.Delahay, *Double Layer and Electrode Kinetics* (Interscience 1965)
6. R.Parsons, *Modern Aspects of Electro-chemistry (no. 1)*, (Butterworths 1954), p. 103
7. D.C.Grahame, *Soviet Electrochemistry (Proc. 4th Conf. Electrochem)*. (Consultants Bureau 1961), *1*, 31
8. J.O'M.Bockris, W.Mehl, B.E.Conway, and L.Young, *J. Chem. Phys., 25* (1956) 776
9. G.C.Barker, *J.Electroanal. Chem., 12* (1966) 495
10. D.C.Grahame and B.A.Soderberg, *J.Chem. Phys., 22* (1954) 449

11. R.Parsons, *Adv. Electrochem. Electrochemical Engng., 1* (1961) 1
12. M.A.V. Devanathan and B.V.K.S.R.A.Tilak, *Chem. Revs., 65* (1965) 635
13. A.Frumkin, *Trans. Symp. Electrode Proc., Philadelphia 1959* (Wiley 1961) p. 1.
14. B.Baron, P.Delahay and D.J.Kelsh, *J.Electroanal. Chem., 18* (1968) 184
15. D.C.Grahame, *J.Amer. Chem. Soc., 79* (1957) 2093
16. D.C.Grahame and R.Parsons, *J.Amer. Chem. Soc., 83* (1961) 1291; supplementary tables of data supplied by authors.
17. C.A.Barlow, *Physical Chemistry — An Advanced Treatise* (Academic Press 1970), *vol. IXA (Electrochemistry),* ch. 2
18. A.Frumkin, *Adv. Electrochem. Electrochemical Engng., 1* (1961) 65
19. A.Frumkin, *Z. Elektrochem., 59* (1955) 807
20. L.Pospisil and R.deLevie, *J.Electroanal. Chem., 25* (1970) 245
21. F.C.Anson and J.Caja, *J.Electrochem. Soc., 117* (1970) 306
22. F.C.Anson, J.H.Christie and R.A.Ostergang, *J.Electroanal. Chem., 13* (1967) 343
23. F.C.Anson and D.J.Barclay, *Anal. Chem., 40* (1968) 1791
24. G.W.O'Dom and R.W.Murray, *J.Electroanal. Chem., 16* (1968) 327
25. D.J.Barclay and F.C.Anson, *J.Electrochem. Soc., 116* (1969) 438
26. Z.Kowalski and F.C.Anson, *J.Electrochem. Soc., 116* (1969) 1208
27. L.Gierst, *Trans. Symp. Electrode Proc., Philadelphia 1959* (Wiley 1961) p. 109
28. J.E.B.Randles, *Trans. Symp. Electrode Proc., Philadelphia 1959* (Wiley 1961) p. 209
29. H.Gerischer, *Z.Elektrochem., 57* (1953) 604
30. T.Berzins and P.Delahay, *J.Amer. Chem. Soc., 77* (1957) 6448
31. J.H.Sluyters and J.J.C.Oomen, *Rec. Trav. Chim., 79* (1960) 1101
32. C.D.Russell, *J.Electroanal. Chem., 6* (1963) 486
33. D.C.Grahame and B.A.Soderberg, Tech. Rept. No. 14 (ONR Contract N8-onr-66903), Feb. 18, 1954
34. A.N.Frumkin, *Z.Physik. Chem., 164A* (1933) 121
35. V.Levich, *Dokl. Akad. Nauk S.S.S.R., 67* (1949) 309; *Chem. Abstr. 44*: 461b
36. K.Narayanan and S.K.Rangarajan, *Australian J.Chem., 16* (1963) 565
37. H.H.Bauer, *J.Electroanal. Chem., 12* (1966) 64
38. R.Tamamushi and K.Matsuda, *J.Electroanal. Chem., 12* (1966) 436
39. R.deLevie and A.A.Husovsky, *J.Electroanal. Chem., 22* (1969) 29; R.deLevie and L.Pospisil, *J.Electroanal. Chem., 22* (1969) 277
40. P.Delahay, *J.Electrochem. Soc., 113* (1966) 967
41. D.E.Smith, *CRC Critical Reviews in Analytical Chemistry, 2* (1971) 247
42. R.Parsons, *Adv. Electrochem. Electrochem. Eng., 7* (1970) 177

CHAPTER 4

Mass Transport

4.1 Types of Mass Transport

The overall electrochemical reaction involves not only a charge-transfer reaction at the interface and possible adsorption and chemical reaction there, but also the movement of various species from one or both of the bulk phases to and/or from the surface. Consequently, interpretation of experimental observations is usually possible only by taking into account mass-transfer processes as well as interface reactions. In this chapter, some salient features of mass-transfer processes and their influence on electrochemical studies will be discussed.

Mass transport may occur by diffusion, by electrical migration, and by convection. Convection and electrical migration can be avoided, but diffusion cannot. A great deal of the theoretical work that has been done on electrochemical reactions has therefore involved the treatment of diffusion processes, and experiments are often designed in such a way as to make diffusion the sole or overweighing process by which mass transport occurs; even when it is not, the diffusion process still needs to be considered (e.g., the diffusion coefficient is present in the relation for limiting currents at rotated electrodes, Sections 4.3.2, 4.3.3).

Electrical migration is avoided (e.g. in polarography) by the presence of a large excess of an "inert" electrolyte. It is the ions of the latter that chiefly carry the current through the bulk of the solution: even if the electroactive species is charged, very little of the current through the solution is carried by the charged depolarizer since it is present in such small amount — typically, at 1 or 2% of the concentration of the background electrolyte. Many experiments using techniques not necessarily called polarographic nevertheless employ the device of a background electrolyte to avoid movement of the electroactive species under electrical migration. On occasion, the potential difference between bulk and electrode may still be sufficiently great that movement by electric migration, in addition to diffusion, must be considered; such situations have been referred to in Section 3.6.3.

Mass transport by convection is avoided in many cases. With the dropping mercury electrode, the fall of each drop produces some stirring, but not enough to vitiate the assumption that mass transport occurs solely by diffusion — with the exceptions that

(a)   Polarographic maxima are known to be due to convective movements that originate in the mercury or at the mercury-solution interface and are transmitted to the solution.

(b)   The small amount of stirring can be beneficial, in removing from the vicinity of the electrode the layers of solution that are depleted in the electroactive species. The design of capillaries — vertical or horizontal, blunt or fine-tipped, straight or bent — is influenced by this consideration (1).

In some techniques, controlled convection is employed. A high rate of mass transport cannot be achieved if the latter is limited by diffusion in a quiescent solution. Convective movement of the solution decreases the thickness of the layer in which the concentration of the relevant species changes from its value in the bulk phase. As the thickness of this diffusion layer decreases, the rate of diffusion increases and the rate of mass transport to the electrode is thus enhanced. Therefore, where fast mass-transport is desirable, convection is induced by stirring or pumping the solution or by moving the electrode:

(a)   In the deposition of metals, in preparative electrochemistry (synthesis), and for similar purposes, the solution is usually stirred vigorously.

(b)   In electroanalysis, sensitivity can be increased by bringing depolarizer to the electrode more rapidly; thus, rotating electrodes have been used.

(c)   If mass transport is sufficiently fast, the charge-transfer step may become rate-determining and can then be studied. Very high rates of movement of solution have been used to achieve this ("hydrodynamic voltammetry"), but the early work (2) has not been followed up.

(d)   Ring-disc electrodes are now attracting increasing attention. Species formed at a rotating disc-electrode are carried by convection to a ring-shaped electrode surrounding the disc; the rate of movement can be controlled so that the lifetimes of intermediates can be studied.

4.2   Diffusion

4.2.1 Fick's Law

The basic equation for diffusion processes is Fick's Law, which states that the number of molecules crossing a plane at point x at the time t (i.e. the flux of molecules) is directly proportional to the concentration gradient. This is expressed symbolically in the form

$$\text{Flux} = q_{x,t} = D\,\frac{\partial}{\partial x}\,(C_{x,t}) \tag{4-1}$$

where C is the concentration, and D is a proportionality constant and is called the diffusion coefficient. The rate of change with time of the concentration C between parallel planes at point x and $(x + dx)$ equals the difference in the flux at the two planes, so that

$$\frac{\partial}{\partial t}\,(C_{x,t}) = \frac{\partial}{\partial x}\left\{D\frac{\partial}{\partial x}\,(C_{x,t})\right\} \tag{4-2}$$

This expression is known as Fick's Second Law of Diffusion. It is valid for the conditions assumed, namely planes parallel to one another and perpendicular to the direction of diffusion — i.e. for linear diffusion (in contrast with, for example, cylindrical or spherical diffusion where the lines of flux are not parallel but are perpendicular to segments of spheres or cylinders rather than planes).

The diffusion coefficient, introduced as a proportionality factor in equation (4-1), actually depends in magnitude on the environment, including the concentration of the diffusing species. Very frequently, however, this dependence is small; and almost always in electrochemical discussions the diffusion coefficient of a given species is taken to be constant (for a given background solution). Then, equation (4-2) becomes

$$\frac{\partial}{\partial t}\,(C_{x,t}) = D\,\frac{\partial^2}{\partial x^2}\,(C_{x,t}) \tag{4-3}$$

Application of equations (4-1) and (4-3) to particular situations represents a great deal of the work that has been done on mass transport in electrochemistry; some examples are given below. Details can be found elsewhere (3).

4.2.2 Potential-Step Electrolysis

If an electroactive substance is present and a potential is applied such that all molecules of the species are reduced (or oxidized, as the case may be) immediately upon contact with the electrode, the following conditions apply:

At time $t = 0$, the concentration is uniform throughout the system and equals the "bulk concentration", C^B; at later times, the concentration at the electrode surface, $C_{0,t}$, is zero; and the concentration increases as the distance from the electrode increases. In symbols,

$$C_{x,0} = C^B$$
$$C_{0,t} = 0 \text{ for } t > 0$$
$$C_{x,t} \to C^B \text{ as } x \to \infty \tag{4-4}$$

Solution of Fick's Law (for linear diffusion, i.e. a planar electrode) for these conditions gives the flux at the electrode surface as

$$q_{0,t} = C^B\,(D/\pi t)^{1/2} \tag{4-5}$$

and consequently the current flowing is given by

$$i = nFA\,q_{0,t} = nFAC^B\,(D/\pi t)^{1/2} \tag{4-6}$$

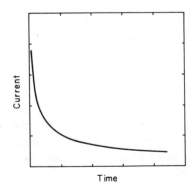

Fig. 4-1. Decay of current with time after application of a potential step.

Thus, the current in such a situation decreases with the square root of time after application of the potential (see Fig. 4-1). It is also proportional to the bulk concentration, to the area of the electrode*, and to the square root of the diffusion coefficient. (According to equation (4-6), the current is instantaneously infinite at time zero. Obviously, in fact only a finite current flows, limited by the nature of the circuit — resistance, capacity, etc. Thus, measurements that reflect the behavior of the electrode process can be made only after some finite time from the beginning of application of the potential. In experiments where one attempts to make measurements at very short times, it is crucial that the influence of the external circuit be properly taken into account. In studies with potential steps, the rise-time of the pulse generator is usually the limiting factor. Quite often in electrochemical work, the reliability of measured quantities depends on proper circuit design and understanding of the properties of the polarizing and measuring circuits).

Equation (4-6) can be used to explain results obtained *under the conditions assumed above:* a fixed surface, depolarizer reacting as soon as it reaches the electrode, initial potential applied "instantaneously" (i.e. "potential-step" electrolysis). The relation must be modified if the potential changes relatively slowly ("potential sweep"), if both oxidized and reduced species coexist at the given electrode potential, and if the area of the electrode varies (as, for example, in polarography).

4.2.3 Polarography

Under polarographic conditions, the electrode potential is changed (during the recording of a polarographic curve) from a value where the oxidized species is stable, through an intermediate region, to a value where the reduced species is stable. The Nernst equation holds at equilibrium and

$$C_{O(0,t)} \mid C_{R(0,t)} = \exp[nF(E-E_c^\circ)/RT] \qquad (4\text{-}7)$$

If equilibrium is to be maintained, the fluxes of the oxidized and reduced species at the electrode surface must be equal, so that

$$D_O \frac{\partial}{\partial x}\left\{ C_O(x,t)\right\}_{x=0} + D_R \frac{\partial}{\partial x}\left\{ C_R(x,t)\right\}_{x=0} = 0 \qquad (4\text{-}8)$$

In addition, the following conditions apply when the bulk of the solution contains only oxidized species, as is usually the case (other situations can of course be treated also):

$$C_O(x,t) \rightarrow C^B ; C_R(x,t) \rightarrow 0 \text{ as } x \rightarrow \infty \qquad (4\text{-}9)$$

Solution of the diffusion equation for these conditions (equations (4-7) to (4-9)) gives

$$i = nFAD_O^{1/2}C^B/\pi^{1/2}t^{1/2}(1+[D_O/D_R]^{1/2}\exp[nF(E-E_c^\circ)/RT]) \qquad (4\text{-}10)$$

or $\quad i = nFAD_O^{1/2}C^B/\pi^{1/2}t^{1/2}(1+[D_O/D_R]^{1/2}[C_O(0,t)/C_R(0,t)]) \qquad (4\text{-}11)$

*Provided the current density across the electrode is uniform — see footnote in Section 2.2.2

This expression reduces to equation (4-6) when the concentration of the oxidized form at the electrode surface is zero at all times, a situation that corresponds to the limiting diffusion current, i_d, in polarography.

Therefore, $\quad i = i_d/(1+[D_O/D_R]^{1/2}[C_O(0,t)/C_R(0,t)])$ (4-12)

or, using equation (4-7) and rearranging,

$$E = E_c^\circ + (RT/nF)\ln(D_R/D_O)^{1/2} + (RT/nF)\ln[(i_d-i)/i]$$ (4-13)

This is the equation for the reversible polarographic wave (see Fig. 4-2), with the half-step potential, $E_{1/2}$, given by

$$E_{1/2} = E_c^\circ + (RT/nF) \ln (D_R/D_O)^{1/2}$$ (4-14)

One also obtains, from solution of the above equations, expressions for the concentrations of the oxidized and reduced species at the electrode surface at any time t, namely

$$C_{O(0,t)} = C^B(i_d-i)/i$$ (4-15)

$$C_{R(0,t)} = C^B(i/i_d) (D_O/D_R)^{1/2}$$ (4-16)

These expressions are useful since they enable one to calculate concentrations at the electrode surface from measurement of the current under polarographic conditions.

So far, no consideration has been given to the fact that, in polarography with the dropping mercury electrode, the assumption of linear diffusion to an electrode of fixed area is not valid. A complete solution of the problem has to take into account:

(a)   that diffusion closely approximates spherical geometry;
(b)   that the surface of the electrode increases with time;
(c)   that the growing drop pushes solution ahead of it;
(d)   that a new drop grows into an already depleted solution;
(e)   convection effects produced by the falling drop.

It turns out that calculation based on spherical rather than on linear diffusion does not usually alter the fit of experiment with theory to a marked extent *except under special circumstances* – e.g., in the consideration of certain effects in alternating

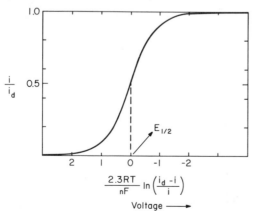

(on this scale, the half-step potential is at zero)   Fig. 4-2. Reversible d.c. polarogram.

64

electrical fields, semi-quantitative or even qualitative predictions based on a linear-diffusion model may be wrong (4). Under conventional polarographic conditions, the treatment given above can be quite satisfactorily applied after two corrections are made — for the fact that the growth of the drop causes a larger concentration gradient, and for the direct increase in electrode area with time.

The first correction results (3) in a predicted current that is greater by a factor of $(7/3)^{1/2}$.

The area of the drop can be calculated given that the rate of flow of mercury, m mg. sec.$^{-1}$, is independent of time t. The drop area, A, is given by

$$A = 4 \pi r^2 \tag{4-17}$$

where r is the radius of the (assumed) spherical drop. The volume of the drop, from geometry and from weight respectively, is given by

$$\text{volume} = (4/3) \pi r^3 = mt/d \tag{4-18}$$

where d is the density of mercury. Substituting,

$$A = 0.85 \ (mt)^{2/3} \tag{4-19}$$

where the magnitude of the density at 25°C has been used.

Thus, the polarographic limiting current is given by the combination of equations (4-6) (i.e. equation (4-11) for C_o=0 at the surface), equation (4-19), and the factor $(7/3)^{1/2}$:

$$i_d = 7.06 \times 10^4 \ nD^{1/2} \ C^B m^{2/3} t^{1/6} \tag{4-20}$$

with i_d in amperes, D in cm^{2}sec.$^{-1}$, C^B in moles/cm^3, m in g/sec and t in sec. This is the so-called Ilkovic equation, and it holds well in most cases. Various modifications of the equation have been proposed (5) to account for some relatively minor discrepancies.

Observation of the way in which current varies with time at the dropping mercury electrode often makes possible identification of the rate-controlling step and of the mode of mass transport.

When diffusion is rate-limiting, the polarographic current is given by equation (4-20), so that

$$i \ (\text{diffusion-controlled}) \propto t^{1/6} \tag{4-21}$$

There are processes in which the electroactive species is not present in the bulk of the solution, but is formed at the electrode in some chemical reaction. If this reaction is rate-determining (a "kinetically controlled" process), then the current will be proportional to the rate of the chemical step, and this in turn is proportional to the area of the electrode which is given by equation (4-19); therefore

$$i \ (\text{kinetically controlled}) \propto t^{2/3} \tag{4-22}$$

Oscilloscopic observation of current-*vs.*-time curves in polarography is a valuable technique. In addition to inferences based on equations (4-21) and (4-22), anomalies observed in such curves can give valuable information about the nature of an electrode process (e.g., see Section 5.4.1 on surfactant effects).

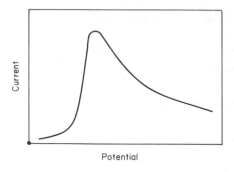

Fig. 4-3. Linear-sweep voltammogram.

4.2.4 Linear-Sweep and Cyclic Voltammetry

When the potential of an electrode is changed at an appreciable rate *(linear-sweep voltammetry)*, peak-shaped curves of current-*vs.*-voltage are obtained (Fig. 4-3). The shape of this curve can be qualitatively understood from the results given earlier:

In the rising portion of the curve, the current is determined by the ratio of oxidized to reduced molecules at the surface; thus, the current increases as the potential is made more cathodic, as in polarography. Once a potential is reached at which all molecules reaching the surface are reduced, the magnitude of the current is limited by the rate of arrival of new molecules: in the absence of convection, or of an expanding electrode, the current therefore decreases with time, as in the case of potential-step electrolysis discussed earlier. Quantitative discussion of curves such as in Fig. 4-3 can be found elsewhere (6).

A useful modification of the linear-sweep method is that of *cyclic voltammetry:* the electrode potential is swept anodically and cathodically on alternate voltage-sweeps. Information about the reversibility of the process, formation of intermediates, and the nature of surface films can often be obtained.

4.3   Convection

4.3.1 Introductory

It has been mentioned that convection can be useful in electrochemical work, for example, where high rates of mass transfer are desired for practical or theoretical reasons. Thus, the sensitivity of analytical procedures can be increased by using convection to enhance the speed of mass transport. In the electrochemical preparation of inorganic and organic substances, rotation of the electrode can increase yields (more so than stirring of the solution by other means), and the relative yields of the products can be varied by changing the speed of rotation (7).

The use of convection does not permit neglect of diffusion, however. Consider the reduction of an ion M^+ at an electrode, without convection and at a potential where the equilibrium concentration of M^+ at the electrode is zero. There exists a concentration gradient close to the electrode, and M^+ moves by diffusion in this gradient. If the solution is now stirred gently, the solution nearest to the electrode (and the walls of the cell) will not move, but adjacent "layers" of solution will move and the region of the solution through which the concentration is uniform will move closer to the electrode: i.e., the thickness of the layer enclosing the concentration gradient (the *diffusion layer*) will decrease, more so as the solution is stirred more vigorously. The current due to reduction of M^+ increases because the diffusion layer is thinner and the concentration gradient steeper; the flux of diffusing substance can be written as

$$\text{Flux} = \frac{D}{\partial} (C^B - C^{el}) \tag{4-23}$$

where ∂ is the thickness of the diffusion layer. Since ∂ depends on the degree of stirring, the flux depends both on the diffusion parameters (D, concentration gradient) and on the variables affecting convection (stirring rate, rotation of electrode).

For example, with a rotating electrode at low speeds of rotation, a typically peak-shaped voltammogram (Fig. 4-3) is obtained when the potential is swept at the usual rates used at stationary electrodes. As the speed of rotation of the electrode is increased, the shape of the curve tends towards a normal polarographic curve (Fig.4-2). The decrease in current after the peak in Fig. 4-3 is due to depletion of the solution in the vicinity of the electrode to an extent greater than could be compensated by the rate of diffusion; however, by rotation of the electrode the thickness of the diffusion layer is decreased and the flux of depolarizer at the electrode becomes larger − in the limiting case, convection keeps the concentration of the depolarizer uniform so close up to the electrode that the current does not fall below that produced when the potential is first applied.

Despite the practical advantages of convective mass-transport in a number of situations, the use of convection has the important drawback that mathematical treatment is difficult; this makes such experiments unattractive in work aimed at quantitative mechanistic and kinetic studies. For instance, when a solution is stirred the diffusion-layer thickness is not usually uniform across the surface, and calculation of the magnitude is complicated. However, there is one type of convection that has been successfully treated mathematically: a rotating disc with laminar (non-turbulent) flow of the solution. This type of electrode is coming to be of increasing importance, and is described below.

4.3.2 Rotating Disc Electrodes

Theoretical discussion of a disc-shaped electrode rotated around its center is conveniently begun by considering the disc to be of infinite extent; later, this condition can be made applicable to practical situations be ensuring that the diameter of the rotating electrode (together with the insulated covering that shields the sides and top of the disc from the solution) is large compared to the thickness of the hydrodynamic layer, i.e. of that part of the solution where convection occurs.

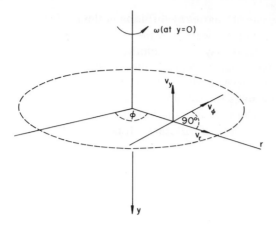

Fig. 4-4. Coordinates and velocity components at a rotating disc (from Riddiford (8), by permission of John Wiley).

It is convenient to use cylindrical coordinates as shown in Fig. 4-4; thus, convection is described by velocities of movement of the solution v_y normal to the disc, v_r radially out from the center of the disc (or from the axis of rotation), and v_ϕ around the axis (i.e. v_ϕ is the angular velocity). It is assumed that the flow of solution is laminar—neighboring layers "slide" past one another without turbulence. Further, it is assumed that the velocity v_y is independent of r, the distance from the axis of rotation. With these assumptions, the dependence of the velocities on rotation speed and other variables can be calculated; details are given by Riddiford (8), and the results are illustrated in Fig. 4-5.

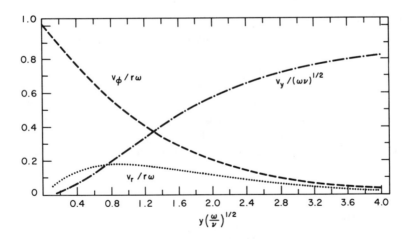

Fig. 4-5. Velocity components at a rotating disc electrode (after Riddiford (8)); ν is the kinematic viscosity of the solution (reproduced by permission of John Wiley).

The angular velocity v_ϕ of the solution is equal to that of the disc for y=0, and decreases with increasing distance from the disc. The velocity normal to the disc,

v_y, is zero at the disc itself and increases to a limiting value with increasing distance from the electrode. The velocity of the solution radially out from the axis of rotation is also zero at the disc (y=0), and increases to a maximum with increasing distance from the electrode, decreasing again to zero sufficiently far from the electrode.

The thickness of the hydrodynamic layer is the distance from the electrode beyond which the solution is no longer rotated by the disc. From Fig. 4-5, v_ϕ at the distance $y=2.8(\nu/\omega)^{1/2}$ is one tenth of its value at y=0, and therefore the magnitude $2.8(\nu/\omega)^{1/2}$ can be taken as a measure of the thickness of the hydrodynamic layer.* It is this quantity that should be small compared to the total diameter of the rotating disc; for a given electrode, this puts a lower limit on the rate of rotation ω that can be used if results are to be in agreement with the theory.

An upper limit on the rate of rotation is set by the condition that the flow of the liquid be non-turbulent. The onset of turbulence is determined not only by the rate of rotation and the viscosity of the liquid but also by the roughness of the surface of the electrode, and by any eccentricity of rotation of the disc on its axis.

The magnitude of the limiting current obtained with a rotating disc is, under these assumptions, given by

$$i_{lim} = 0.62 \ nFAD^{2/3} \ \nu^{-1/6} \omega^{1/2} C^B \qquad (4\text{-}24)$$

Thus, analytical applications are indicated because the current is a measure of the concentration C^B; moreover, the sensitivity can be increased by raising the speed of rotation ω.

Furthermore, the diffusion coefficient D can be calculated since, for a given system of known concentration, all other parameters are known or measurable. This use of a rotating disc-electrode can be compared with use of the polarographic method to determine diffusion coefficients via the Ilkovic equation (4-20). The rotating-disc method is probably to be preferred since equation (4-24) is in more precise agreement with the best experimental data than is equation (4-20) (however, modifications (5) of equation (4-20) can be used); also, the fact that the diffusion coefficient appears to the power 2/3 in equation (4-24) and to the power 1/2 in equation (4-20) makes the limits of uncertainty for the value of D somewhat narrower when the rotating-disc method is used.

The kinetic parameters of the charge-transfer step can be obtained from measurements at a rotating disc (9). Since mass transport is faster than in conventional polarography with diffusion control, systems with higher exchange-currents can be studied; the technique has a capability comparable to that of the faradaic-impedance method.

Practical aspects, particularly the shape of the rotated electrode and its covering, have been discussed by Riddiford (8).

Equation (4-24) can be regarded as arising from diffusion in a concentration gradient whose thickness is given by

$$\partial \doteq 1.8 \ D^{1/3} \nu^{1/6} \omega^{-1/2} \qquad (4\text{-}25)$$

---

* ν is the kinematic viscosity of the solution

This expression demonstrates that the thickness of the diffusion layer is inversely proportional to the square root of the rotation rate, with a consequent increase in the rate of mass transport.

4.3.3 Ring-Disc Electrodes

The products of the reaction at a disc electrode move away from the axis of rotation of the disc, and it should be possible to detect them with a suitable device. One such device is the ring-disc electrode, where a ring electrode surrounds the disc (in the same plane as the disc). The disc and ring are connected to separate polarizing and measuring circuits, so that electroactive products of the reaction at the disc can be detected electrochemically at the ring electrode.

In recent years, theory has been developed for the magnitude of the ring current for various types of reaction occurring at the disc, and application has been made to the detection of intermediates formed at the disc, and to the measurement of rates of reactions involving these intermediates. Qualitatively, it is clear that the amount of a species arriving at the ring will depend on the rate at which the species reacts as it moves from the disc, where it is formed, to the ring. Quantitative treatments have been published for the reaction schemes shown in Table 4-1.

Table 4-1. Reaction sequences discussed theoretically for the ring-disc electrode (from Albery and Bruckenstein (10) by permission of Faraday Society)

Reaction at disc electrode	Reaction in solution	Reaction at ring electrode	ref.
$A \rightarrow B$	nothing	$B \rightarrow A$ l.c.	11
rev. $A \rightleftarrows B$	nothing	$B \rightleftarrows A$ rev.	12
$A \overset{k'}{\rightarrow} B \rightarrow P$	nothing	$B \rightarrow Q$ l.c.	11, 13
$O \rightarrow B$	$B + A \rightarrow P$	$B \rightarrow Q$ l.c.	14
$O \rightarrow B$	$B + A \overset{k}{\rightarrow} P$	$B \rightarrow Q$ l.c.	15
$O \rightarrow B$	$B \overset{k}{\rightarrow} P$	$B \rightarrow Q$ l.c.	16
rev. $G \rightleftarrows B$	$B \overset{k}{\rightleftarrows} A$	$B \rightleftarrows G$ rev.	10
$A \overset{k'}{\underset{k'}{\rightleftarrows}} B$	nothing	$B \overset{k'}{\underset{k'}{\rightleftarrows}} A$	10

l.c., assumes limiting current is being passed; rev., electrode couple assumed to be reversible; k, indicates that kinetic terms for this reaction are included in the treatment.

Work on rotating discs and on ring-disc electrodes is expanding rapidly as this is being written, and new developments of significance are likely to arise. The contemporary literature should be consulted for information in this area; a comprehensive literature survey in this area has been published by Adams (17).

4.4 References

1. I.Smoler, *Collection Czech. Chem. Commun., 31* (1966) 703; and references given there.
2. J.Jordan, R.A.Javick, and W.E.Ranz, *J. Amer. Chem. Soc., 80* (1958) 3846
3. P.Delahay, *New Instrumental Methods in Electrochemistry* (Interscience 1954)
4. J.R.Delmastro and D.E.Smith, *Anal. Chem., 38* (1966) 169
5. J.M.Markowitz and P.J.Elving, *Chem. Revs., 58* (1958) 1047
6. R.S.Nicholson and I.Shain, *Anal. Chem., 36* (1964) 706
7. H.V.K.Udupa and B.B.Dey, *Proc. 6th Mtg. C.I.T.C.E., Poitiers 1954* (Butterworths 1955) p. 87
8. A.C.Riddiford, *Adv. Electrochemistry Electrochem. Engng., 4* (1966) 47
9. D.Jahn and W.Vielstich, *J.Electrochem. Soc., 109* (1962) 849
10. W.J.Albery and S.Bruckenstein, *Trans. Faraday Soc., 62* (1966) 2596
11. W.J.Albery and S.Bruckenstein, *Trans. Faraday Soc., 62* (1966) 1920
12. W.J.Albery, S.Bruckenstein, and D.T.Napp, *Trans. Faraday Soc., 62* (1966) 1932
13. V.G.Levich, *Physicochemical Hydrodynamics,* (Prentice-Hall 1962)
14. W.J.Albery, S. Bruckenstein, and D.C. Johnson, *Trans. Faraday Soc., 62* (1966) 1938
15. W.J.Albery and S.Bruckenstein, *Trans. Faraday Soc., 62* (1966) 2584
16. W.J.Albery and S.Bruckenstein, *Trans. Faraday Soc., 62* (1966) 1946
17. R.N.Adams, *Electrochemistry at Solid Electrodes* (Dekker 1969)

CHAPTER 5

Adsorption Processes

5.1   Observed Phenomena

5.1.1 Behavior of Uncharged Surface-Active Species

In this chapter, adsorption processes are considered other than those involved in setting up the double-layer in the solution of a "simple" electrolyte, which were discussed in Chapter 3. The systems to be considered comprise such an electrolyte but in addition another, surface-active, substance; the latter is usually present in relatively small amounts in the bulk of the solution. Of interest here are the changes produced by the surface-active substance.

Many uncharged species show a tendency to become adsorbed at an electrode-solution interface. This results in changes of the interfacial tension and of the capacity of the electrical double-layer. Typically, the change in surface tension in the presence of a surface-active substance (*surfactant* or *tenside*) is as shown in Fig. 5-1.

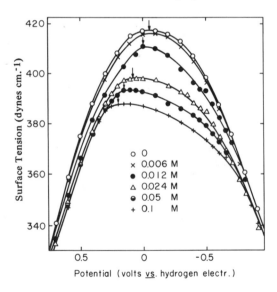

Fig. 5-1. Electrocapillary curves for n-amyl alcohol at different molar concentrations in 1M sodium perchlorate and 0.001M perchloric acid. Arrows indicate points of zero charge; from Breiter and Delahay (1) (reproduced by permission of American Chemical Society).

It is apparent that the surfactant affects the surface tension only within a certain range of potentials, around the potential of zero charge. The inference is clear that only within this range of potentials is the surfactant actually adsorbed — the Gibbs adsorption equation (3-1) shows that the change of surface tension upon addition of a species to the solution can be zero only if the surface excess of that species is also zero (equation 3-9)).

In the absence of surfactant, the solution considered is an electrolyte in some solvent. At the surface, cations and anions are present as a result of electrostatic forces as well as of possible specific adsorption; in addition, the solvent molecules may be oriented in some fixed way, or statistically, in the vicinity of the surface. Adsorption of the surfactant can be expected to displace some ions and some solvent molecules from the surface. With increasing concentration of surfactant, the surface tension decreases progressively at a fixed potential as solvent and ions are progressively displaced from the surface; and the potential range over which the tenside is adsorbed increases, since the attraction between electrode and electrolyte ions can be overcome at progressively higher charges on the electrode as the adsorbability of the tenside increases.

The charge on the electrode as a function of potential and of surfactant concentration is shown in Fig. 5-2. The charge decreases in the presence of adsorption because of the displacement

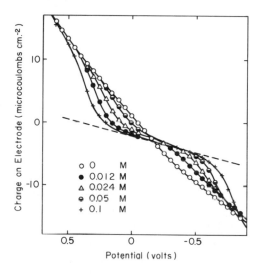

Fig. 5-2. Variation of charge on the electrode with potential for the solutions of Fig. 5-1; from Breiter and Delahay (1) (reproduced by permission of American Chemical Society).

of the ions: the charge on the electrode is always equal in magnitude (though opposite in sign) to that on the solution side of the double layer, so that a decrease in the latter bespeaks a corresponding decrease in the former. The charge on the electrode is related to the surface tension by the Lippmann relation (equation (3-11)): where the electrocapillary curves are decreased in slope by adorption of surfactant (Fig. 5-1), the charge (positive or negative) on the electrode is correspondingly less.

Fig. 5-3 shows the differential capacity as a function of potential and of concentration of surfactant. These curves can be inferred from Fig. 5-1 or Fig. 5-2 because of the thermodynamic relationship between surface tension, charge, and differential capacity (equations (3-11), (3-13), (3-14)).

In terms of a model of the electrode-solution interface, the decreased capacity in the presence of adsorption (around the e.c.m.) can be ascribed to a lowering of the

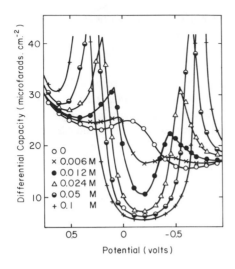

Fig. 5-3. Differential-capacity-versus-potential curves for the solutions of Fig. 5-1; from Breiter and Delahay (1) (reproduced by permission of American Chemical Society).

dielectric constant and to an increase in the distance between the "plates" of the double-layer "capacitor". Since the dielectric constant of water is high, replacement by any other substance will produce a decreased capacity of the double layer*. Adsorption of tenside will also increase the distance between the electrode surface and the outer Helmholtz plane, since the layer of adsorbate is thicker than a layer of water for virtually any adsorbate encountered in practice.

At the potentials where adsorption gives way to desorption, capacity peaks (also termed *tensammetric waves*) are seen (Fig. 5-3). This is readily understood since the capacity is low at smaller polarizations (positive or negative to the e.c.m.) and high at larger polarizations: since the differential capacity is measured with an alternating-voltage signal, peaks of *differential* capacity must result — the rate of change with potential of the *static* capacity is large at the desorption potentials. From a thermodynamic point of view, these peaks follow from the shape of the curves of charge *vs.* potential (Fig. 5-2) and the fact that the differential capacity is the derivative of charge with respect to potential.

The region of adsorption increases with concentration of the tenside. Empirical equations relating the potentials of the capacity peaks to concentration of tenside have been given:

$$E = a + b \log C \tag{5-1}$$

$$E^2 = a' + b' \log C \tag{5-2}$$

These different relationships are reconciled in one theory of adsorption (Section

---

* This argument is not entirely foolproof, since dielectric saturation occurs in the intense electric field at the inner double-layer, and the dielectric constants of water and of other substances in this environment are not known; the extrapolation from bulk properties involves a degree of uncertainty. The recent suggestions that water can perhaps exist in a state ("anomalous water", "polywater") that has physical properties different from normal water is also of interest in this connection, since "anomalous water" — if it does indeed exist — is apparently formed at surfaces (or in capillaries).

74

5.3), which predicts a parabolic relationship: equations (5-1) and (5-2) then correspond to limited ranges of potential and concentration only.

Generally, the region of adsorption decreases as the temperature increases, but the opposite can happen with surfactants whose solubility decreases with increasing temperature. The desorption peaks are at least approximately equidistant from the e.c.m.; how exact this relation might be remains unknown in view of a lack of precise and comprehensive data. The desorption peaks indicate the replacement of surfactant by solvent and by ions of the background electrolyte—cations at potentials cathodic to the e.c.m., and anions at anodic potentials. Since these ions are generally specifically adsorbed to varying degrees, one would not expect the desorption peaks to be exactly symmetrical around the e.c.m. A recent study (2) has indeed shown that the peak potentials of the anodic waves are markedly affected when the background electrolyte is changed, whereas the cathodic peaks are affected very little, in keeping with the fact that anions usually show specific adsorption whereas inorganic cations are rarely specifically adsorbed to any pronounced extent.

Since adsorption involves displacement of ions, one might expect that increasing the concentration of the background electrolyte would lead to decreased adsorption of a tenside. The opposite effect is sometimes observed, however: thus, the results in Table 5-1 appear

Table 5-1. Region of Adsorption (between tensammetric wares) as a function of Concentration of Amyl Alcohol (from Bauer et al. (3) by permission of Elsevier)

Concentration of Alcohol	Salt Solution					
	KF		Na_2SO_4		KCl	
	0.1M	1M	0.1M	1M	0.1M	1M
0.01M	810mV	770mV	740mV	920mV	620mV	550mV
0.02	1033	954	903	1078	788	745
0.03	1100	1070	990	1170	900	860
0.04	1218	1154	1071	1211	950	902
0.05	1270	1210	1120	1220	1020	960
Saturated	1577	1420	1436	1315	1463	1345
Apparent Adsorption Coefficients at e.c.m. (liters moles^{-1})						
	37.0	60.9	64.1	147	34.8	18.9

to show that amyl alcohol is decreasingly adsorbed when the concentration of potassium chloride or potassium fluoride is increased, but the opposite — anomalous — effect is seen in sodium sulfate. The apparent anomaly arises through the neglect of activity changes; salts affect the solubilities of surfactants, as well as being competitively adsorbed. When the results are compared at constant activity of alcohol (Table 5-2) rather than at constant concentration, the anomalies disappear. (There is also no anomaly in the saturated alcohol solutions in Table 5-1: saturated solutions have equal activities of the alcohol). These results can be interpreted in terms of competitive adsorption and the relative surface-activities of the salts ($KF < Na_2SO_4 < KCl$).

Table 5-2. Region of Adsorption as a function of Activity of Amyl Alcohol (from Bauer et al. (3) by permission of Elsevier)

Activity of Alcohol	KF		Salt Solution Na$_2$SO$_4$		KCl	
	0.1	1M	0.1M	1M	0.1M	1M
0.079	986mV	757mV	858mV	748mV	768mV	606mV
0.143	1132	914	988	876	908	748
0.224	1254	1038	1098	979	1020	862
0.316	1342	1132	1178	1056	1105	948
1.0	1577	1420	1436	1315	1463	1345
Adsorption Coefficients Corrected for Activity Changes						
	34.3	30.1	55.4	35.5	32.5	11.5

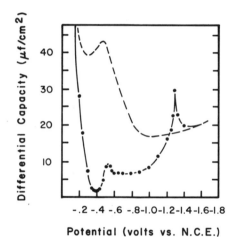

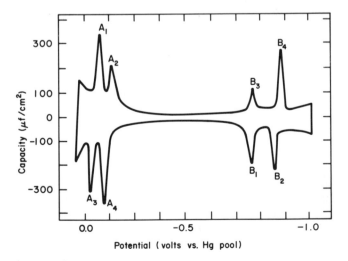

Fig. 5-4. Saturated solution of n-octyl alcohol in 1M KCl. The minimum around -0.4 V is ascribed to multilayer adsorption (from Melik-Gaikazyan (4); reproduced by permission).

Fig. 5-5. Saturated solution of n-C$_8$H$_{18}$OH in 1M KI. The double desorption peaks are ascribed to formation of multilayer adsorbed films (from Loveland and Elving (5); reproduced by permission of American Chemical Society).

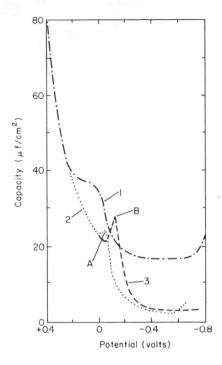

Fig. 5-6. Reorientation peaks (A,B) with adsorption of surfactant on both sides of the peak; 1- 0.1M HCl; 2- 0.1M HCl plus 10^{-3}M α-naphthoquinoline; 3- 0.1M HCl plus 10^{-3}M β-naphthoquinoline (from Fischer (6); reproduced by permission).

In some cases, observations have been reported that differ in type from those illustrated in Fig. 5-1 to 5-3. For instance, appreciable variation of the capacity within the region of adsorption, and double desorption peaks, have been found, and ascribed to the presence of multilayers of adsorbate (Fig. 5-4, 5-5). Usually, however, the generalizations made in this section are valid for uncharged substances, with the important exception of aromatic compounds; the latter may show behavior also found with anionic species (see below), as for instance only a cathodic desorption peak and apparently no desorption as the potential is made progressively more anodic. Sometimes, a peak is seen that is in the region of prevailing adsorption, i.e. there is adsorption of the surfactant at both more anodic and at more cathodic potentials (e.g. Fig. 5-6). Such a peak may reflect a reorientation of the surfactant at that potential – in the example shown, it is likely that the surfactant is adsorbed with the molecules perpendicular to the interface at cathodic potentials and with the molecules flat at anodic potentials (see below).

5.1.2 Behavior of Charged Surfactants

Uncharged tensides are displaced from the surface both at sufficiently negative and at sufficiently positive charges on the electrode. However, if the tenside is itself a cation, one often does not see replacement by the cations of the background electrolyte even at very negative charges (Fig. 5-7c). The curves of surface tension and of differential capacity are then unsymmetrical, showing adsorption across the whole

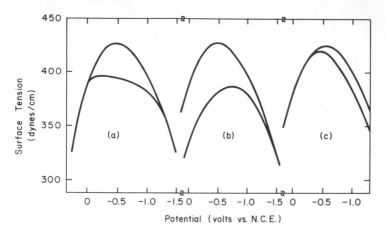

Fig. 5-7. Electrocapillary curves: (a) 1N Na_2SO_4 and 1N Na_2SO_4 + 0.1M $C_5H_{11}OH$; (b) 1N Na_2SO_4 and 1N Na_2SO_4 + 1M pyrogallol; (c) 1N H_2SO_4 and 1N H_2SO_4 + 0.1N $[(C_2H_5)_4N]OH$; from Frumkin and Damaskin (7) (by permission of Butterworths).

cathodic branch of the curves as well as in a part of the anodic, with a single desorption potential on the anodic branch. Conversely, anionic surfactants usually show desorption only on the cathodic side of the e.c.m. Aromatic compounds often behave like anionic species in this respect (Fig. 5-7b); it is thought that the aromatic molecules in these cases are adsorbed with the plane of the aromatic ring parallel to the surface, so that the π-electrons interact with the positively charged electrode surface in a way that is similar to the interaction between an anion and the positive surface.

5.1.3 Mixtures of Surfactants

When two uncharged surfactants are present in the same solution, the observed behavior is often the same as in a solution that contains only that surfactant which is adsorbed over the wider range of potentials. For instance, in Fig. 5-8 there is illustrated the appearance of only single cathodic desorption peaks in mixtures of surfactants: the peak of octanol is replaced by that of cyclohexanol, which in turn is replaced by that of methyl cellulose.

However, phenomena observed in the presence of several surfactants can be more complicated than this. Thus, Fig. 5-9 shows *gradual* replacement of one surfactant by another: the desorption peak of triethylphosphate (TEP) at -1.1 V is gradually lowered as increasing amounts of polyethylene glycol (PEG) are added; the adsorbate at potentials more positive than -1.1 V is purely TEP at first, then presumably partly TEP and partly PEG (see also Fig. 5-10); between -1.1 and -1.7 V, only PEG is adsorbed. Similarly (Fig. 5-10), when increasing amounts of TEP are added to a solution containing PEG, the desorption peak of the latter (at ca. -1.75 V) is unaffected. However, at potentials more positive than ca. -1.0 V, PEG is progressively displaced

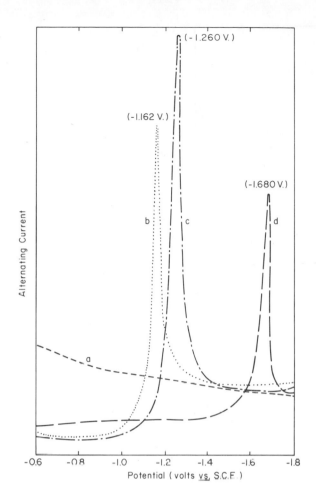

(-1.260 V.)

(-1.162 V.)

(-1.680 V.)

b

a

c

d

Alternating Current

-0.6   -0.8   -1.0   -1.2   -1.4   -1.6   -1.8

Potential (volts vs. S.C.F.)

Fig. 5-8. Influence of tensammetric waves on one another: (a) 0.1N KCl (supporting electrolyte); (b) saturated octyl alcohol in 0.1N KCl: (c) same as (b) + 0.1M cyclohexanol; (d) same as (c) + 0.1 per cent methyl cellulose (after Breyer and Hacobian (8), by permission of Commonwealth Scientific and Industrial Research Organization, Australia).

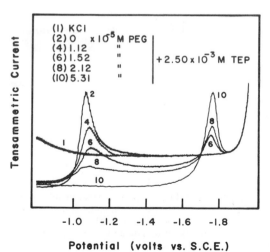

(1) KCl
(2) 0 $\times 10^{5}$ M PEG
(4) 1.12   "
(6) 1.52   "   + 2.50 $\times 10^{-3}$ M TEP
(8) 2.12   "
(10) 5.31   "

1

2

4

6

8

10

10

8

6

Tensammetric Current

-1.0   -1.2   -1.4   -1.6   -1.8

Potential (volts vs. S.C.E.)

Fig. 5-9. Mixtures of triethylphosphate and polyethylene glycol; from Jehring (9) (by permission of Elsevier).

79

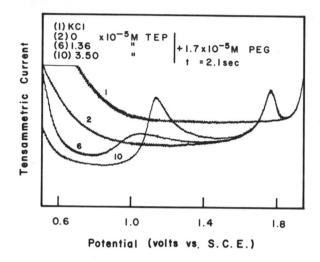

Fig. 5-10. Mixtures of triethylphosphate and polyethylene glycol; from Jehring (9) (by permission of Elsevier).

by TEP and a "desorption" peak appears at ca. -1.1 V, corresponding to replacement of TEP by PEG as the potential is made more cathodic. Thus, it is not only the adsorbability of the surfactant around the e.c.m. that governs the variation of adsorption with potential — different surfactants show different rates of change of adsorbability with changing electrode potential.

When measurements are made with a dropping mercury electrode, another variable is of importance: the drop-time of the electrode. Measurements are commonly made at the end of the growth of each drop, and the magnitude of the differential capacity (or of the tensammetric current) reflects the situation at that time. At short drop-times, a surfactant whose molecules are relatively small and rapidly diffusing may then cover the surface even if the solution contains a surfactant with greater adsorbability (larger adsorption coefficient) if the latter diffuses relatively slowly; at longer drop-times, the situation may then be reversed — cf. Fig. 5-11.

In systems containing a charged and an uncharged tenside, one usually sees adsorption of both species in different regions of potential. For instance, an anionic

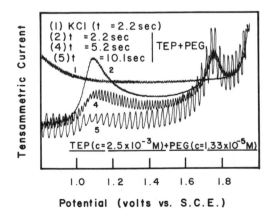

Fig. 5-11. Drop-time effect in solutions containing two surfactants; from Jehring (9) (by permission of Elsevier); 2.5×10^{-3} M triethylphosphate and 1.33×10^{-5} M polyethylene glycol.

80

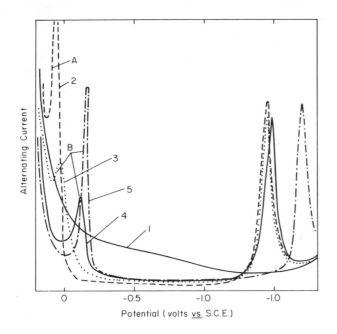

Fig. 5-12. Tensammetric peak of cyclohexanol (A) and peaks (B) for displacement of cyclohexanol by chloranilate anion at anodic potentials; 1- supporting electrolyte; 2- electrolyte plus 0.15M cyclohexanol; 3- as 2, plus 10^{-6} M chloranilate; 4- as 2, plus 10^{-5} M chloranilate; 5- as 2, plus 10^{-4} M chloranilate; from Breyer and Bauer (10) (reproduced by permission of Commonwealth Scientific and Industrial Research Organization, Australia).

surfactant is adsorbed at a positively charged electrode; as the charge is made less positive, the anion is replaced by the uncharged surfactant; at sufficiently negative charge, the latter is desorbed (Fig. 5-12). Little work has yet been done on systems containing more than one surface-active species, and one can expect novel and interesting phenomena to be discovered as such studies are made.

5.2   Measurement of Adsorption

It follows from the phenomena described above that adsorption can be measured from observations of charge or of differential capacity, as well as from measurements of surface tension. Charge is not a conveniently measurable quantity, and thus the choice falls between measurement of surface tension and of differential capacity. Both methods have been used, and each has its own advantages and disadvantages. In addition, optical and radio-tracer methods have been used for direct observation of the surface in the presence of adsorption; these methods are described in Sections 7.5 and 7.6. Adsorption can also be measured indirectly by the effects produced on faradaic processes (see Section 5.4.1). A recent review (11) deals specifically with methods of measuring adsorption at electrodes.

Measurement of surface tension involves the observation of quite small changes in tension, and the potentials at which adsorption gives way to desorption are commonly not accurately identifiable (cf. Fig. 5-1). On the other hand, it is usually possible to ensure that the adsorption reaction is at equilibrium (aspects of the experimental technique are described in Section 7.2). The amount adsorbed is calculable by application of the Gibbs adsorption equation in a form like equation (3-9),

81

but it must be recalled that surface excesses so obtained are relative, not absolute, quantities; and that these quantities refer to the whole discontinuity around the interface, not necessarily to a monolayer at the surface. Therefore, calculations of surface area per adsorbed molecule must be accompanied by a recognition that such calculations involve an assumption about the spatial distribution of the adsorbed molecules in the vicinity of the surface, usually that a monolayer is formed.

Measurements of differential capacity permit the desorption potentials (the capacity peaks) to be located quite precisely. On the other hand, calculation of the amount of substance adsorbed depends on the establishment of equilibrium and, in the case of differential-capacity measurements, this means not only that the overall reaction must be at equilibrium but also that the frequency of the electrical signal used in the measurement should be sufficiently low that the adsorption-desorption reaction can follow the changes in the applied field; quite frequently this condition can be achieved only by extrapolation of the results to zero frequency (however, measurements extrapolated to infinite frequency can also, in principle at least, be used for determination of the amount of tenside adsorbed (12)).

An uncertainty exists in attempting to relate differential-capacity values directly to the degree of coverage, θ, of the surface. Frequently, the following relationship is used

$$C_M = C_0 \ (1-\theta) + C_3 \theta \qquad\qquad (5\text{-}3)$$

where C_M is the measured capacity at surface coverage and C_0, C_S are the capacities at $\theta = 0$ and $\theta = 1$ respectively. This equation is based on a model that regards the total capacity as composed of two capacities in parallel. Such a model seems appropriate as a first approximation, but exact calculations may require a more detailed model that takes into account the various regions of the double layer (13,78). However, equation (5-3) is quite commonly applied, in the absence of a suitable alternative.

Calculation of surface coverage or surface concentration does not conclude the problem of obtaining measurements that can be readily interpreted. The influence of the electric field at the surface is of importance, and one has the choice of measuring adsorption at *constant charge on the electrode* or at *constant potential*. The adsorption isotherm obtained depends on this choice, and discussion continues (14,78) on the relative merits of the two approaches. The first is based partly on the analogy to adsorption studies at uncharged surfaces, where the potential across the interface may vary and isotherms are used that ignore this; the analogy to measurements at the e.c.m. is direct. On the other hand, work at constant potential is more convenient and isotherms of reasonably simple form have been found to describe many of the results obtained.

5.3   Theory of Adsorption Processes

Theories of adsorption at electrodes are not in a particularly satisfactory state at the present time, despite the fact that a considerable amount of work in this area has been carried out. Almost invariably, these theories have dealt with the matter as if the reaction consisted only of the adsorption and desorption of a species from the surface, whereas in actuality the reactions involve the displacement of some species by another. When the tenside is desorbed, it is replaced by molecules of the solvent and by ions of the electrolyte, and these latter species must affect the energy of adsorption and other parameters of the reaction. In addition, there are not only attractive forces between the adsorbed molecules and the electrode, but also attractive or repulsive interactions laterally between the adsorbed molecules. One aspect of the question, whether to take isotherms at constant charge or at constant potential, is equivalent to a decision about which of these conditions leads to a mathematically simpler expression of these corollary forces.

The most well-known adsorption isotherm is probably that of Langmuir:

$$\theta = \frac{BC}{1+BC} \tag{5-4}$$

where B is an adsorption coefficient and C the bulk concentration of adsorbate. This isotherm is shown graphically in Fig. 5-13.

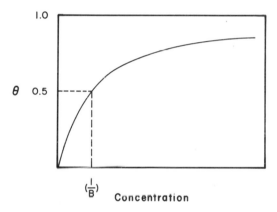

<table>
<tr><td>θ</td></tr>
</table>

Fig. 5-13. Langmuir isotherm; at C = 1/B, θ = 0.5

Although the Langmuir isotherm has often been applied to adsorption processes, many situations where it is not applicable have been observed. The isotherm was derived on the assumption that adsorbed molecules do not interact with one another. A more general treatment, in which an interaction parameter (a) was introduced to account for such possible interactions, led to the Frumkin isotherm

$$BC = [\theta/(1-\theta)] \exp[-2a\theta] \tag{5-5}$$

Here, a is positive when the lateral interaction is one of attraction, and negative in the case of repulsion; when a is zero, this expression reduces to the Langmuir isotherm. As a matter of experience, the interaction parameter is often dependent on the electrode potential. The Frumkin isotherm is illustrated graphically in Fig. 5-14. As was mentioned earlier, in some cases it becomes necessary to replace the concentration in equation (5-5) by the activity of the surfactant (see Tables 5-1 and 5-2 and the relevant discussion).

Parameters obtained by fitting a Frumkin isotherm to experimental data have given

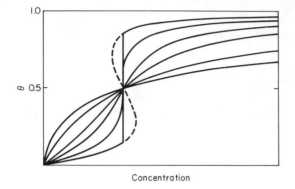

Concentration

Fig. 5-14. Frumkin isotherm; for values of $a \leqslant 0$, the curve is similar to the Langmuir isotherm; for $2 > a > 0$, the curve is S-shaped; for $a \geqslant 2$, a vertical discontinuity appears on the curve; (from Frumkin and Damaskin (7); reproduced by permission of Butterworths).

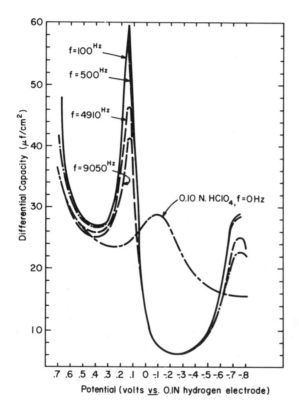

Fig. 5-15. Frequency dependence of differential capacitance at the interface mercury $-0.1N$ $HClO_4$ + 0.031 M n-amyl alcohol; from Hansen et al. (15) (reproduced by permission of American Chemical Society).

plausible values for a range of substances*. In addition, the theory has been applied to the shape of capacity peaks, and values for the interaction parameter can be obtained by studying these peaks; commonly, the value of the interaction parameter obtained from the nature of the peak is in good agreement with the value obtained by measuring the decrease of the capacity near the potential of zero charge. However, the magnitude of the capacity in the region of the peaks is strongly dependent

* Details regarding statements such as this can be found in the review by Frumkin and Damaskin (7), in the monograph by Damaskin et al. (78), and in the references given there.

84

on the frequency of the measuring signal used (e.g., Fig. 5-15); this aspect has not yet been satisfactorily treated theoretically, though some semi-quantitative conclusions have been drawn, from the frequency-dependence, about the rate-determining step in the overall process (diffusion, adsorption, "crystallization" or reorientation of the molecules in the adsorbed film).

Theory based on the Frumkin isotherm predicts a variation of the potentials of the desorption peaks as a function of concentration in a parabolic fashion as shown in Fig. 5-16. This is in accordance with the two types of empirically reported relations,

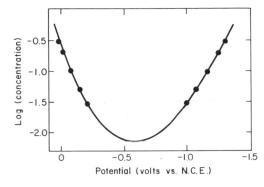

Fig. 5-16. Theoretical dependence of potentials of capacity peaks on concentration and experimental points for t-amyl alcohol in 1M KF (from Frumkin and Damaskin (7); reproduced by permission of Butterworths).

equations (5-1) and (5-2): at large concentrations, E(peak) varies linearly with log C and equation (5-1) fits the observed results, at smaller concentrations the relationship is non-linear and can be fitted to equation (5-2).

Most of the points discussed in this section are relevant to adsorption processes that are at equilibrium (the dependence of the heights of the tensammetric waves on frequency of the a.c. measuring signal, however, indicates that the kinetics of the process is important). Generally, equilibrium conditions can be attained experimentally. Even where a dropping mercury electrode is used, adsorption equilibrium is often attained at potentials between the desorption peaks (a useful test for equilibrium in this situation is that the measured capacity should be independent of the drop-time of the electrode). However, calculations have shown that, particularly in very dilute solutions of strongly surface-active substances, the time required to attain equilibrium may be appreciable — minutes or tens of minutes (16).

The rate of an adsorption-desorption process may be limited by the desorption step itself, by mass transport of the surfactant, or by some other step in the overall sequence — e.g. formation of an oriented layer. Studies of adsorption kinetics have been made by several workers, mainly by examining the frequency dependence of the capacity peaks. In several cases, it was concluded that the adsorption process was diffusion controlled, e.g. for several alkyl alcohols at mercury (17); on the other hand, evidence has been presented that an association of adsorbed molecules may have a rate-determining effect in the case of some of the larger alcohols and fatty acids (18).

Comparatively little work has been carried out on adsorption kinetics, and it appears that no useful generalizations can be drawn at this stage; the reader is referred to

85

the current literature. A full discussion of the theory of adsorption at electrodes, with emphasis on the theory described above, has been given by Frumkin and Damaskin (7) and by Damaskin et al. (78).

A number of other isotherms (apart from those of Langmuir and Frumkin) have been invoked by various workers. No attempt will be made here to survey this whole area, but mention should be made of an isotherm that takes into account the fact that adsorption at electrodes is actually the displacement of solvent molecules by adsorbate. The Flory-Huggins isotherm is based on this idea, and has the form

$$BC = r\theta/(1-\theta)^r \tag{5-6}$$

where r molecules of solvent are displaced by each molecule of surfactant. This equation can be extended to take into account interaction between the adsorbed molecules:

$$BC = [r\theta/(1-\theta)^r]\exp[-2a\theta] \tag{5-7}$$

While this isotherm has been applied in a number of cases (e.g., adsorption in mixed solvent systems (19)), the adsorption of some of the lower alkyl alcohols from aqueous solution is described better (20) by the Frumkin isotherm, i.e. equation (5-7) with r = 1.

The question of adsorption isotherms and related problems has been addressed by Parsons in a recent review (21) that also provides a good survey of the relevant literature.

5.4 Effects of Surfactants on Faradaic Processes

5.4.1 Nature of Possible Effects

Surfactants may affect electrochemical processes in a number of ways. For instance, in polarographic studies, one may find maxima to be suppressed and polarographic steps distorted in shape, shifted in potential, or split into two separate steps. No matter what measuring technique is used, some effect is usually observed that can be attributed to a slowing down of the rate of the electrochemical reaction (however, *increases* in the rate of some step are also sometimes observed).

The interpretation of such surfactant influences is not usually straightforward. An electrochemical reaction consists of a series of steps (Section 2.1), which are affected in different ways (or not at all) by a given surfactant. The effect on the *overall* process then depends on which step or steps is influenced by the surfactant (in particular, whether the affected step was rate-limiting or not), as well as on the interaction of the affected step with reactions coupled to it. Therefore, elucidation of the action of a surfactant requires that knowledge be available of the mechanisms of the process in the absence and in the presence of surfactant, and that the rates of the individual steps be known — at least in relative terms.

However, there are not many electrochemical processes whose mechanism is fully understood, and this paucity of knowledge is even more the case for processes involving foreign* surfactants. Therefore, the following is, to a degree, theoretical and speculative.

The presence of a surfactant may influence one of the steps in the overall process, i.e. mass transport, the charge-transfer step, a chemical reaction preceding or following charge transfer, the adsorption of reactant or product species; and/or a new step may be introduced — penetration of a film of the surfactant may be necessary for charge transfer to occur, and such penetration may be the slowest step in the overall process.

These possible effects are discussed in the following sections; reactions involving adsorbed reactants are treated in Section 5.5. Catalysis of electrode reactions, which may involve surfactant species, is mentioned in Section 6.5; topics relevant to solid electrodes in particular, e.g. the influence of surfactant species on the process of electrocrystallization, are also discussed in Chapter 6.

It may be mentioned that the influence of surfactants on faradaic processes can be, and has been, used as a way of studying the adsorptive behavior of the surfactants; this possibility should be remembered in relation to the discussion in Sections 5.4.2 to 5.4.5. An example is the use of polarographic current–$vs.$–time curves during the life of a single mercury drop (at constant potential): in the presence of surfactants that completely block the faradaic process at the potential in question, and

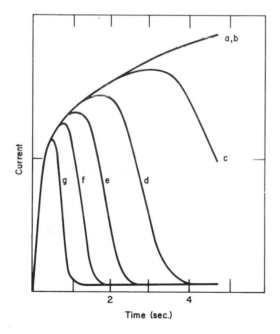

Fig. 5-17. Polarographic current-time curves for faradaic process inhibited by surfactant. Reduction of copper(II) at -0.6 V vs. S.C.E. in presence of Triton X-100 at concentration of : a - 0%; b - 0.001%; c - 0.0015%; d - 0.002%; e - 0.0025%; f - 0.003%; g - 0.004%; from Schmid and Reilley (77) (reproduced by permission of American Chemical Society).

---

* By "foreign" surfactants we mean substances that are not reactants in the overall process being studied, i.e. they are not a starting material nor a product. They may on occasion play a chemical role as intermediates, though presently one tends to look first for a physical role in elucidating inhibitory effects.

where adsorption of the surfactant is diffusion-controlled, curves are obtained as those shown in Fig. 5-17. The surface of the mercury drop, at short times, is not covered by surfactant and the faradaic reaction proceeds normally; at a time t', when sufficient surfactant has diffused to the electrode, the faradaic process is blocked. The time t' is related to the surface concentration (Γ) of surfactant by (22)

$$t' = 1.82 \times 10^6 \ \Gamma^2/DC^2 \tag{5-8}$$

where D is the diffusion coefficient and C the bulk-phase concentration. Thus, measurement of t' enables calculation of Γ (given knowledge of D and C). Since the area of the mercury drop is also readily determined (equation (4-19)), the surface area occupied per molecule of surfactant can also be calculated. The accuracy of this type of calculation is limited by the assumption that blocking of the reaction occurs suddenly when the surface is fully covered. This is not likely to be true in practice, and indeed the curves in Fig. 5-17 show that inhibition of the faradaic process sets in over a finite period of time. It has recently been shown (23) how the accuracy of the calculation can be improved by measuring the effect of the surfactant on the double-layer capacity at the electrode.

5.4.2 Effects on Mass Transport

One thinks of the effects of surfactants almost automatically as resulting from adsorption at the interface. However, it is important that one be aware of the possibility that a surfactant may have other effects.

For instance, the presence of proteins in aqueous solution decreases the polarographic limiting current due to the reduction of a number of substances (metal ions, organic substances such as azo-dyes). This effect was at first ascribed to adsorption of protein onto the electrode with a consequent decrease in the effective area of the electrode and thus a decreased current. However, it was later shown that this explanation is wrong. In point of fact, the depolarizers were forming complexes with the protein in the bulk of the solution, and the rate of mass transport was reduced because the diffusion coefficient of the protein-depolarizer complex was much smaller than that of the free depolarizer − thus, the polarographic diffusion current was lowered. Yet, the proteins used are without doubt surface-active; in fact, the mercury drops do not coalesce when they come together at the bottom of the electrolysis cell, presumably because they are covered with a protein film. Apparently, however, this film formation has no appreciable effect on the course of the polarographic reduction − the influence on mass transport due to complex formation is the reason for the changed polarographic behavior (24).

The use of surfactants to suppress polarographic maxima is another case where mass transport is influenced. Maxima ("streaming maxima") are due to swirling of solution in the vicinity of the dropping mercury electrode, leading to an increased current because of convective mass-transport. Very small amounts of surfactants effectively suppress these anomalous increases in current. It is believed that the surfactants are adsorbed at the dropping electrode and counteract in some way the movement of the mercury-solution interface which, transmitted to the solution, produces the convection. The suppression (or decrease in magnitude) of polarographic maxima is a sensitive test for surface-active substances.

5.4.3 Effects on the Charge-Transfer Step

The charge-transfer step is usually described by the rate constant and the transfer coefficient, and the present question is how these parameters might be affected by the presence of foreign surfactants. There is little reliable data available on this matter because of the problem of obtaining actual values of these kinetic parameters from the apparent, or measured, quantities.

In order to calculate "true" values, possible double-layer effects need to be allowed for; and so the potential distribution in the double layer must be determined in the presence as well as in the absence of surfactant. For situations where specific adsorption of ions is not involved, the potential at the outer Helmholtz plane can be calculated from diffuse-double-layer theory and the capacity of the inner layer, which is small and virtually independent of potential in the presence of an adsorbed film. The results of such a calculation are shown in Fig. 5-18, which may be compared with Fig. 3-7 for the absence of an adsorbed layer. If calculations such as these are used, it must be realized that

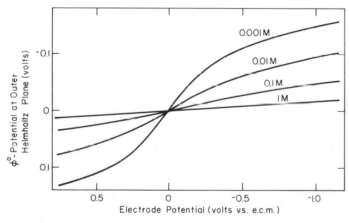

Fig. 5-18. Calculated potential of the outer Helmholtz plane assuming the inner-layer capacity to be 4 μf cm^{-2} and no specific adsorption (T = 25°C) (after Parsons (12); reproduced by permission of John Wiley).

adsorption usually produces a change in the potential of zero charge, so that zero volts on the rational scale of potentials used in Fig. 3-7 and 5-18 does not necessarily correspond to a fixed value of the applied or measured experimental electrode potential. Consequently, one cannot directly obtain from these figures an estimate of the change of ϕ° due to adsorption; in fact ϕ° is not necessarily decreased (by adsorption) at a fixed electrode potential — a shift in the point of zero charge may more than compensate for the lowered capacity of the inner layer.

The complications involved, and the relatively recent recognition of the necessity of making double-layer corrections, are reflected by the paucity of reliable data on the influence of surfactants on charge-transfer kinetics. Aramata and Delahay (25) found that the Frumkin correction (see Section 3.6.2) gives plausible results for the reduction of zinc in the presence of amyl alcohol in supporting electrolytes of magnesium and of barium perchlorates, but not in sodium or aluminum perchlorates possibly because the assumption of a single outer-Helmholtz-plane is reasonable only when the cation of the supporting electrolyte has a similar size (Mg^{++}, Ba^{++}) to that of the reduced species (Zn^{++}). Corrected values for the rate constant were independent of the degree of surface coverage (θ) in the presence of n-amyl alcohol, but not in the presence of thymol or cyclohexanol.

Corrected rate-constants that are independent of θ indicate that the surfactant "blocks" a fraction θ of the surface but influences the reaction at the uncovered surface only *via* changes in the potential distribution in the double layer. Such an effect has been reported for the reduction of Cd^{++} in the presence of butanol (26), n-amyl alcohol (27) and hexyl alcohol (27), and for the reduction of Ti(IV) in the presence of n-amyl alcohol or cyclohexanol (28).

On the other hand, corrected rate-constants that are functions of θ bespeak a more complicated process than physical blocking of the surface. Such results have been reported for the reduction of Ti(IV) in the presence of thymol (28), for the reduction of zinc in the presence of thymol or cyclohexanol (29) (contrast the effect of n-amyl alcohol in this system (25), see above), for the reduction of Cd(II) in the presence of leucoriboflavin (30), and for the reduction of chromate ion in the presence of n-amyl alcohol (31).

When the surfactant is a charged species, the effect on charge-distribution in the double layer is pronounced even at small values of θ. It has been reported in several such cases that the surfactant influence at small θ can be explained by the charge effect and that at large θ a physical blocking effect is observed: thus, the reduction of chromate ion is accelerated in the presence of small amounts of tetraalkylammonium salts and hindered as the concentration of the organic cation is increased (32); reduction of VO_2^+ is accelerated by small amounts, and hindered by large amounts, of dodecylsulfonate (33).

5.4.4 Effects on Chemical Reactions

The influence of surface-active substances on the reduction of polyvalent cations has been regarded by some workers (34) as being caused by a hindering of a chemical disproportionation step. The reduction of, for instance, a divalent cation was thought to proceed according to

$$M^{++} + e \rightarrow M^+ \tag{5-9}$$

$$2M^+ \rightarrow M^{++} + M(\text{electrode}) \tag{5-10}$$

and surfactants were thought to hinder step (5-10) primarily. This interpretation was disputed by other investigators (35). More recently, the original theory appears to have been substantiated in studies (36) of the effect of phenol and of gelatin on the reduction of Cd(II).

In the reduction of organic nitrocompounds, it is generally accepted that the first charge-transfer step involves a single electron, leading to formation of a radical anion. The latter may undergo further reduction, or may disproportionate. The reduction of m-nitrophenol has been examined in some detail (37). It was found that the presence of small amounts of alcohols enhances the observed faradaic admittance and splits the d.c. polarographic step (Fig. 5-19). Apparently,

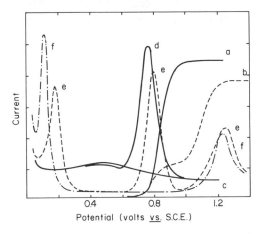

Fig. 5-19. Reduction of m-nitrophenol, effect of alcohol: 10^{-3}M nitrophenol; d.c. polarograms in absence of alcohol (a) and with 10% t-butanol added (b); a.c. polarograms corresponding are (d) and (e); (c) is the base current, (f) background electrolyte plus butanol (from Britz and Bauer (37), by permission).

only one electron is transferred per molecule at the potential where, in absence of alcohol, four electrons are transferred; and the rate of acceptance of that electron is enhanced in the presence of alcohol. By analysis of the faradaic impedance as a function of frequency and amount of alcohol added, it was shown that the reaction in absence of alcohol involves the reduction of adsorbed nitrophenol; a one-electron reduction step is followed by two competing paths for further reduction — disproportionation of the reduction product, or further reduction in a two-electron step. Upon the addition of small amounts of alcohol, the nitrophenol is displaced from the surface, and the disproportionation is hindered, while the further reduction of the initial product ceases (to occur at a more negaitve potential, as shown by the d.c. polarogram). Thus, the presence of the surface-active alcohol makes the reduction of nitrophenol proceed *via* a less complex reaction path. When larger amounts of alcohol are present, the rate of the initial reduction is decreased as less of the surface becomes available for the process.

Reduction of maleic acid is controlled by the rate of addition of protons to the anion before charge transfer. This pre-protonation occurs both in the bulk of the solution and at the surface; Afanasev (38) has reported that the protonation reaction at the surface is hindered in the presence of alcohols.

It has thus been established in several instances that surfactants influence chemical steps in the overall electrochemical process, and it seems that such an effect may be of quite widespread occurrence.

5.4.5 Penetration of an Adsorbed Film

In some cases, an adsorbed film causes an electrode process to cease altogether, at any rate until the electrode potential is increased; one can then think in terms of a physical barrier to the approach of the depolarizer to the electrode surface. In other cases, however, a faradaic reaction may continue to proceed at a "fully covered" surface, albeit at a slower rate. For instance, polarographic currents have been observed that are, over a wide range of potentials, lowered from the diffusion-controlled magnitude to one that presumably reflects the rate of penetration of the adsorbed film (Fig. 5-20).

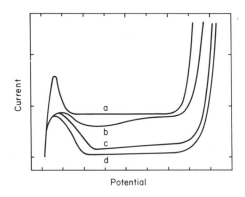

Fig. 5-20. Current-voltage curves for the deposition of Bi(III) on a dropping mercury electrode from 1N H_2SO_4 (aq.) with additions of tribenzylamine: (a) no addition, (b) $1.5 \times 10^{-4}M$, (c) $3 \times 10^{-4}M$, (d) $6 \times 10^{-4}M$ (selection of data from Fig. 4 in Kryukova and Loshkarev in Trudy Soveshchaniya po Elektrokhimii, Moscow, 1953, p. 276 by Parsons (12), reproduced by permission of John Wiley).

It seems that the adsorbed film may have holes or pores that permit limited access of depolarizer to the electrode surface. It would then be expected that, for a given film, the rate of the faradaic process would depend on the size of the depolarizer. This may explain the observation (28), for example, that adsorption of thymol (for $\theta >$ ca. 0.8) strongly blocks the reduction of cadmium ions in citrate media, but not in chloride media where the reduced species has a smaller physical size.

A faradaic process taking place in pores in an adsorbed film will be affected not only by the relative sizes of pore and depolarizer, but also by the different electrical and chemical environment compared to that at a "wide" patch of uncovered surface. Thus, the electrical double-layer effect will be different; and one would also expect that the rates of chemical reactions coupled to the charge-transfer step would depend on the size of the pore in which the reaction occurs. Thus, in the case of a process that involves disproportionation following the addition of an electron, the disproportionation rate would decrease when the pore size is so small that two depolarizer molecules are not likely to be present at the same time.

Interesting in this connection is the work of Kastening (39), who calculated the area per molecule of inhibitor and of depolarizer for a number of systems (Table 5-3). It is noteworthy that the area apparently required by the depolarizer may change according to the nature of the inhibitor. The change appears to be small for the charged depolarizer species (nitrobenzene anion, methyl orange) and very marked for the uncharged aminoazobenzene; this might be explained in that the charged species will

Table 5-3. Area Requirements of Inhibitors and Depolarizers (after Kastening (39), by permission of Bunsengesellschaft)

Inhibitor		Depolarizer		
		p-nitrochlorobenzene radical anion	Methyl orange	p-aminoazobenzene
—		49 Å^2/molecule	53 Å^2/ molecule	72 Å^2/molecule
Benzonitrile	24 Å^2/molecule	72	53	94
p-Tolunitrile	31	62	74	189
Diphenylsulf-oxide	45	54	34	90
Tylose SL600	550	55	55	193

have a strongly preferred orientation relative to the charged electrode surface whereas the uncharged species may more readily assume various orientations according to the nature of the environment produced by the film of inhibitor.

5.5 Adsorbed Reactant Species*

5.5.1 General

Adsorption of the reactants represents a possible step in an electrochemical reaction. As with any other step, adsorption may be rate-controlling, and/or it may alter the effective concentration of the species at the site of the reaction. In addition, the energy change in the reaction can be affected: the energy difference associated with the reaction

$$0 \rightleftharpoons R \qquad (5\text{-}11)$$

will, in general, be different from the energy changes associated with

$$0 \text{ (adsorbed)} \rightleftharpoons R \qquad (5\text{-}12)$$
$$\text{or } 0 \text{ (adsorbed)} \rightleftharpoons R \text{ (adsorbed)} \qquad (5\text{-}13)$$
$$\text{or } 0 \qquad \rightleftharpoons R \text{ (adsorbed)} \qquad (5\text{-}14)$$

Consequently, one may observe one of the processes (5-11 to 5-14) at a certain electrode potential but another at a different potential. In other words, processes involving reactant adsorption may proceed *via* different pathways at different potentials. It has also been suggested that in some cases two pathways may both be effective at a given potential. Generally, one assumes that for weak adsorption the process involving adsorbed reactant occurs at essentially the same potential as in the absence of adsorption, and that for strong adsorption an appreciable difference of potential exists for the different pathways. For instance (in the classical example of reactant adsorption in the polarographic literature), methylene blue is reduced in two polarographic steps (see Section 5.5.4, Fig. 5-22); at the

---

* The term "adsorbed reactant(s)" will be used here for adsorption of starting material and/or product.

more positive wave the process involved is (5-14), at the more negative wave it is thought to be (5-11). The difference in potential corresponds to the energy of adsorption of the reduced species (leucomethylene blue). As another example, the expected effect of reactant adsorption as observed in cyclic voltammetric studies is shown in Fig. 5-21.

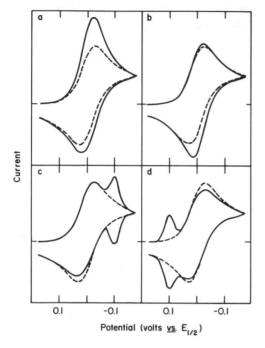

Fig. 5-21. Theoretical cyclic voltammograms for cases involving adsorption a, reactant adsorbed weakly; b, product adsorbed weakly; c, reactant adsorbed strongly; d, product adsorbed strongly. Dashed lines indicate behavior for the uncomplicated Nernstian charge transfer; (after Wopschall and Shain (40); reproduced by permission of American Chemical Society).

Historically, investigators' attitudes to the phenomenon of reactant adsorption have differed somewhat depending on whether mercury electrodes or solid electrodes are involved. In polarographic work, effects resulting from adsorption of reactants were systematically studied at a comparatively late stage in the development of the field as a whole, and the phenomena concerned were regarded as "anomalous". It has only quite recently become apparent that systems involving adsorption of reactants are not at all uncommon; not only is adsorption often found with organic species, but also quite frequently with inorganic cations as well as anions.

On the other hand, studies at solid electrodes have long focused on the adsorption of reactants as a (or *the*) point of prime importance in the electrochemical process. This is particularly the case with the hydrogen-evolution reaction, which has been the subject of innumerable investigations.

It is this difference in approaches that has influenced the discussion of reactant adsorption separately for mercury and for solid electrodes in subsequent sections.

94

5.5.2 Observation of Reactant Adsorption

The same techniques can be used to investigate adsorption of reactants as for the study of adsorption processes in general — electrocapillary methods, measurements of double-layer capacity. In addition, however, reactant adsorption can be studied more or less indirectly from observation of the faradaic behavior of the species involved, using suitable methods.

The appearance of separate "adsorption waves" in polarography has been mentioned in Section 5.5.1, and the effects of reactant adsorption in cyclic voltammetry were illustrated there.

In a.c. studies (a.c. polarography, faradaic-impedance measurements) possible effects of reactant adsorption have been generally described by modifications of the equivalent electrical network for processes without adsorption; there is no general agreement on this matter, and the original literature (41-45) should be consulted for details. Unusual sensitivity of the a.c. method has been ascribed to adsorption of the species concerned, and anomalous temperature effects can be similarly explained (46).

Chronocoulometry (47) is a comparatively new technique in which one measures the charge passed following a step-jump in potential. This technique is a very convenient one for the study of adsorbed reactants, since the charge passed "instantaneously" through reaction of adsorbed ions or molecules can be separated by extrapolation from the charge passed as a result of the reaction of ions or molecules that move to the surface during the time interval of the experiment. Much of the data on the adsorption of reducible inorganic cations has been gathered by this method.

Generally speaking, effects due to reactant adsorption will be observable by a number of different techniques, and no single method is preeminently suitable. Non-electrochemical methods that aim at a direct measure of adsorbed species are likely to prove invaluable in providing information not otherwise obtainable — e.g., regarding the type of bonding between adsorbent and adsorbate. The development of such methods is discussed in Sections 7.5 and 7.6.

5.5.3 Reactant Adsorption at Mercury — Inorganic Species

The specific adsorption of inorganic species was briefly mentioned in Sections 3.5 and 3.6.1. It is generally agreed that anions are specifically adsorbed, particularly at positively charged mercury — with the possible exception of F^-. Oxidation or reduction of anions under these conditions therefore involves a faradaic process with adsorbed reactants. In the discharge of the halide ions (48), the product of the reaction is a mercury salt which is itself adsorbed.

In recent years, evidence has accumulated that a number of inorganic cations are also adsorbed at mercury electrodes. Often, however, the adsorption of cations is observed only in the presence of specifically adsorbed anions, or is strongly enhanced in those situations. It may be, therefore, that the observed specific adsorption of anions arises from "squeezing out" of the anions from the aqueous phase and/or specific interactions between the anions and mercury; whereas the reported specific adsorption of inorganic cations may result from attraction to specifically adsorbed anions, to ion-pairing with the latter, and/or to adsorption in the form of "salt molecules" or ion pairs. Thus, adsorption of cadmium has been observed in the presence of halides or thiocyanate (43, 49-52); but no adsorption was found in nitrate (51), sulfate or perchlorate (52), nor in 1M NH_4OH plus 1M NH_4Cl (43). In the presence of halides, adsorption has been observed not only of cadmium but also of lead (43, 53-55), thallium (43), bismuth (43), tin(II) (43), and copper(I) (43). Indium (56) and zinc (57) are adsorbed in thiocyanate medium, but not in chloride (43). Adsorption of thallium has been reported not only in halide (43) media but also in nitrate and sulfate (58-61). Complexes of cobalt (41, 62) and copper (63) with organic ligands show adsorption phenomena.

Yet more examples are available, and it is to be expected that future work will deal increasingly with the adsorption of inorganic cations now that the phenomenon has been well established in a number of instances. Hopefully, more understanding of the nature of the adsorbed species and of the forces involved will result. The formation of complex ions or ion-pairs in the double layer also needs to be further understood in relation to the influence of double-layer structure and potential-distribution on faradaic processes (Section 3.6).

5.5.4 Reactant Adsorption at Mercury — Organic Species

The classical example of reactant adsorption is in the reduction of methylene blue, studied polarographically by Brdicka (64, 65). Fig. 5-22 shows that, at concentrations of methylene blue below ca. 6×10^{-5} M, a single step is observed, while at higher concentrations a second step appears at more negative potentials. The first step corresponds to reduction of unadsorbed methylene blue to adsorbed leucomethylene blue; the height of this step is limited, not by the rate of diffusion of methylene blue, but by the surface available for adsorption of the reduced molecules. Such steps are now called "prewaves", "adsorption steps", or "Brdicka prewaves". The second step is observed when the surface is fully occupied by leucomethylene

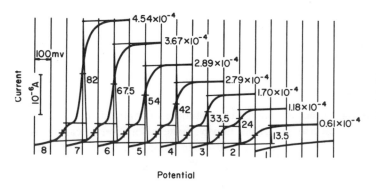

Fig. 5-22. Polarographic curves of methylene blue at pH = 7.96 showing the anomalous wave, the height of which is independent of the concentration, from Brdicka (65) (reproduced by permission).

blue, and requires a more negative potential since the reduced form finds itself in a higher energy state (unadsorbed as opposed to adsorbed). A recent study by cyclic voltammetry (66) has elucidated further details of the reduction mechanism, including the fact that methylene blue itself is adsorbed.

Adsorption phenomena have been observed with many organic species, and it may be that adsorption is *usually* involved in aqueous solutions of organic compounds. In partly or wholly non-aqueous media, adsorption phenomena may be less frequently observed due to the higher solubility of most organic substances in such media.

For details of the observed effects and their elucidation, the current literature should be consulted; some of the other compounds examined include thiourea (67), quinone (46, 68), chloranilic acid (10, 69), cystine (70), nitrophenol (37), riboflavin (71, 72), perinaphthenone (73), flavin mononucleotide (74), azobenzene (75), benzoyl pyridines (76).

Reactant adsorption at solid electrodes is discussed in Chapter 6.

5.6   References

1. M.Breiter and P.Delahay, *J.Amer. Chem. Soc., 81* (1959) 2938
2. A.K.Shallal, Ph.D.Thesis, University of Kentucky (1969)
3. H.H.Bauer, H.R.Campbell, and A.K.Shallal, *J.Electroanal. Chem., 21* (1969) 45
4. V.I.Melik-Gaikazyan, *Zhur. Fiz. Khim., 26* (1952) 1184
5. J.W.Loveland and P.J.Elving, *J. Phys. Chem., 56* (1952) 935
6. H.Fischer, *Wiss. Z. Techn. Univ. Dresden, 15* (1966) 435
7. A.N. Frumkin and B.B.Damaskin, *Modern Aspects of Electrochemistry no. 3* (1964) 149
8. B.Breyer and S.Hacobian, *Australian J. Sci. Res., A5* (1952) 500
9. H.Jehring, *J.Electroanal. Chem., 21* (1969) 77
10. B.Breyer and H.H.Bauer, *Australian J. Chem., 8* (1955) 472
11. H.H.Bauer, P.J.Elving, and P.Herman, *Modern Aspects of Electrochemistry,* in press
12. R.Parsons, *Adv. Electrochemistry Electrochem. Engng., 1* (1961) 1
13. R.Parsons, *Trans. Faraday Soc., 55* (1959) 999
14. R.Parsons, *J.Electroanal. Chem., 8* (1964) 93; and references given there
15. R.S.Hansen, D.J.Kelsh, and D.H.Grantham, *J. Phys. Chem., 67* (1963) 2316
16. P.Delahay and C.T.Fike, *J.Amer. Chem. Soc., 80* (1958) 2628
17. For example, A.Frumkin and V. I. Melik-Gaikazyan, *Dokl. Akad. Nauk S.S.S.R., 77* (1951) 855; *Chem. Abstr. 45:* 6909e
18. For example, W.Lorenz, *Z.Elektrochem., 62* (1958) 192
19. J.Lawrence and R.Parsons, *J.Phys. Chem., 73* (1969) 3577
20. A.K.Shallal, H.H.Bauer and D.Britz, *Coll. Czech. Chem. Commun., 36* (1971) 767
21. R.Parsons, *Rev. Pure Appl. Chem., 18* (1968) 91
22. J.Koryta, *Coll. Czech. Chem. Commun., 18* (1953) 206
23. P.W.Board, D.Britz and R.V.Holland, *Electrochim. Acta, 13* (1968) 1633
24. B.Breyer and H H.Bauer, *Australian J. Chem., 6* (1953) 332
25. A.Aramata and P.Delahay, *J.Phys. Chem., 68* (1964) 880
26. H.Jehring, *Polarography 1964* (Macmillan 1966), vol. 1, p. 349
27. W.Müller and W.Lorenz, *Z. Physik. Chem., 27* (1961) 23
28. P.Delahay and I.Trachtenberg, *J. Amer. Chem. Soc., 80* (1958) 2094
29. P.Delahay, *Double Layer and Electrode Kinetics* (Interscience 1965), p. 233
30. T.Biegler and H.A.Laitinen, *J.Electrochem. Soc., 113* (1966) 852
31. P.Delahay and E.Solon, *J.Electroanal. Chem., 11* (1966) 233
32. L.Gierst, J.Tondeur, R.Cornelissen, and F.Lamy, *CITCE Meeting, Moscow 1963;* quoted in reference 29, p. 229
33. J.Kuta and J.Weber, *Electrochim. Acta, 9* (1964) 541
34. For example, J.Heyrovsky, *Faraday Soc. Disc., 1* (1947) 212
35. A.N.Frumkin, *Dokl. Akad. Nauk S.S.S.R., 85* (1952) 373; *Chem. Abstr. 46:* 10956i

36. B.Lovrecek and N.Marincic, *Electrochim. Acta, 11* (1966) 237

37. D.Britz and H.H.Bauer, *Electrochim. Acta, 13* (1968) 347

38. B.N.Afanasev, *Soviet Electrochemistry, 1* (1965) 1302

39. B.Kastening, *Z.Elektrochem., 68* (1964) 979

40. R.H.Wopschall and I.Shain, *Anal. Chem., 39* (1967) 1514

41. H.A.Laitinen and J.E.B.Randles, *Trans. Faraday Soc., 51* (1955) 54

42. M.Senda and P.Delahay, *J.Phys. Chem., 65* (1961) 1580

43. G.C.Barker, *Trans. Symp. Electrode Processes, Philadelphia 1959* (Wiley 1961) 325

44. P.Delahay, *J.Electroanal. Chem., 19* (1968) 61

45. A.M.Baticle and F.Perdu, *J.Electroanal. Chem., 12* (1966) 15

46. B.Breyer and H.H.Bauer, *Australian J. Chem., 8* (1955) 467

47. F.C.Anson, *Anal. Chem., 38* (1966) 54

48. T.Biegler, *J.Electroanal. Chem., 6* (1963) 357, 365, 373

49. G.W.O'Dom and R.W.Murray, *Anal. Chem., 39* (1967) 51

50. F.C.Anson, J.H.Christie, and R.A.Osteryoung, *J.Electroanal. Chem., 13* (1967) 343

51. G.Lauer, R.Abel, and F.C.Anson, *Anal. Chem., 39* (1967) 765

52. A.Hamelin, *Compte Rend., C262* (1966) 520

53. R.W.Murray and D.J.Gross, *Anal. Chem., 38* (1966) 392

54. G.C.Barker and J.A.Bolzan, *Z.Anal.Chem., 216* (1966) 215

55. M.Sluyters-Rehbach, B.Timmer, and J.H.Sluyters, *J.Electroanal. Chem., 15* (1967) 151

56. B.Timmer, M.Sluyters-Rehbach, and J.H.Sluyters, *J.Electroanal. Chem., 15* (1967) 343

57. R.A.Osteryoung and J.H.Christie, *J. Phys. Chem., 71* (1967) 1348

58. M.Sluyters-Rehbach, B.Timmer, and J.H.Sluyters, *Rec. Trav. Chim., 82* (1963) 553

59. A.M.Baticle and F.Perdu, *J.Electroanal. Chem., 13* (1967) 364

60. A.Frumkin, *Trans. Symp. Electrode Processes, Philadelphia 1959* (Wiley 1961) 1

61. B.Baron, P.Delahay and D.J.Kelsh, *J. Electroanal. Chem., 18* (1968) 184

62. F.C.Anson, *Anal. Chem., 36* (1964) 932

63. E.Jacobsen and G.O.Kalland, *Acta Chem. Scand., 21* (1967) 905

64. R.Brdicka, *Z.Elektrochem., 48* (1942) 278

65. R.Brdicka, *Collection Czech. Chem. Commun., 12* (1947) 522

66. R.H.Wopschall and I.Shain, *Anal. Chem., 39* (1967) 1527

67. B.Case and F.C.Anson, *J. Phys. Chem., 71* (1967) 402

68. W.Lorenz and U.Gaunitz, *Collection Czech. Chem. Commun., 31* (1966) 1389

69. S.Roffia and E.Vianello, *J.Electroanal. Chem., 15* (1967) 405

70. T.Biegler and B.Breyer, *Rev. Polarog. (Kyoto), 7* (1959) 31

71. T.Biegler and H.A.Laitinen, *J.Phys. Chem., 68* (1964) 2374

72. Y.Asahi, *J.Pharm. Soc. Japan, 76* (1956) 378

73. B.Breyer and H.H.Bauer, *Australian J. Chem., 8* (1955) 480

74. A.M.Hartley and G.S.Wilson, *Anal. Chem., 38* (1966) 681

75. B.Nygard, *Ark. Kemi, 26* (1966) 167

76. J.Volke and M.M.Amer, *Collection Czech. Chem. Commun., 29* (1964) 2134

77. R.W.Schmid and C.N.Reilley, *J.Amer. Chem. Soc., 80* (1958) 2087

78. B.B.Damaskin, O.A.Petrii and V.V.Batrakov, *Adsorption of Organic Compounds on Electrodes* (Plenum Press 1971)

CHAPTER 6

Solid Electrodes

6.1 Introductory

Much of the material in earlier chapters, particularly on the double layer and adsorption, represents concepts and understanding that arose from work with mercury
electrodes, chiefly in fact the dropping mercury electrode. In part, this results from
the history of studies of the electrode-solution interface: until the mid-1930's, there
was no agreement as to how this interface could be represented by an equivalent
electrical circuit. Conflicting conclusions were reached by various workers, on the
basis of apparently conflicting experimental data. There were two difficulties: firstly,
the distinction between polarized and reversible electrodes had not been clearly
made, and a single representation was sought for electrode behavior irrespective
whether faradaic current was passing or not; secondly, the extreme sensitivity of
many measurements to traces of surface-active impurities had not been realized. It
was the introduction by Grahame (1) of the dropping mercury electrode into measurements of double-layer capacity that led to the concept that, in the absence of
faradaic processes, the interface behaves like an electrical capacitor without leakage
resistance over a wide range of frequencies. The dropping mercury electrode over-
came the problem of contamination of the working electrode, after contact with the
electrolyte, by progressive accumulation of impurities at the surface.

Nowadays, careful purification of experimental systems has been described that
makes reliable measurements with non-renewed electrode surfaces feasible, but the
available data is not extensive. The question remains, to what degree our understanding of the electrical double-layer at mercury can be validly used in considering
other electrode systems.

Liquid (mercury) electrodes are physically smooth and homogeneous, chemically
uniform, and to a great degree chemically inert. Much progress has been made by
ignoring chemical interactions, or at least by remaining with operational descriptions
of the systems where specific adsorption of ions, or adsorption of other surfactants,
is involved. Characteristically, such adsorption process at mercury are reversible and
fast, and can be conveniently regarded as perturbations of the "normal" capacitive
double-layer consisting of a featureless conductor of electronic charge in contact
with an electrolyte.

On the other hand, processes at solid electrodes are characteristically influenced by
chemical interactions. Intermediate species may exist over wide ranges of potential,
strongly bound to the electrode, e.g. adsorbed hydrogen atoms or atoms of a reducible cation. Solid electrodes can frequently be removed from the solution with adsorbents remaining on the surface in (at least approximately) quantitative amounts,
indicating that strong chemical bonds are involved in the adsorption process.

A great deal of work at solid electrodes has had as an implicit assumption that there exists an electrical double-layer similar to that at an ideally polarized mercury electrode, and a number of supposedly inert electrode materials have been studied in attempts to confirm this; however, at the present time, the question remains open. Solid electrodes almost invariably form surface films involving oxygen at anodic potentials in aqueous solution, and adsorbed hydrogen at cathodic potentials, leaving only a small intermediate range of potentials where an "ideal" double layer might subsist; whether it actually does remains to be seen. At any rate, over large ranges of potentials, the double layer at solid electrodes is certainly influenced by film formation, and specific adsorption is likely to be a more crucial influence than with mercury electrodes.

Thus, electrochemistry at solid electrodes presents problems that are not necessarily encountered in polarography and related work. Some of these matters are briefly discussed in the following sections. A monograph dealing specifically with electrochemistry at solid electrodes has recently appeared (2). It is vitally necessary that progress be made in the understanding of processes at solid electrodes, since most electrochemical work in fact has to be done with solid electrodes − e.g. in the areas of electroplating, electrowinning and refining, design and manufacture of batteries and fuel cells.

6.2 Characterization of Solid-Electrode Surfaces

The surface of a solid electrode is determined by inherent characteristics − the composition of the material, its crystallographic nature, the homogeneity (or otherwise) of the exposed surface. Moreover, the surface is very prone to change with time, due to progressive accumulation of substances from solution (by adsorption and/or electrochemical deposition) and/or by corrosive processes. Finally, the geometry of the electrode is of importance at two levels; at the level of molecular dimensions, and also on a macroscopic scale since the distribution of current across the surface depends on this, and local polarization effects may ensue.

The first criterion one seeks to meet is reproducibility of results. With solid electrodes, this is often a matter of some difficulty. Two aspects of the problem can be distinguished: the nature of the surface of the electrode itself, and possible contamination of the surface upon contact with the electrolyte. It is now well known that conventional analytical-reagent grade chemicals usually contain sufficient impurities to significantly contaminate an electrode surface quite rapidly. For instance, observed charge-transfer rate-constants can decrease enormously within fractions of a minute after exposure of the surface to the solution (cf. Table 6-1).

Purification of solutions is therefore a prerequisite for obtaining reproducible results at solid electrodes. The degree of purification required depends on the nature of the investigation. Diffusion-controlled processes may not demand special efforts (see Section 6.4) whereas studies of heterogenous rate-constants generally do. Two types of impurities have to be considered: electroactive and surface-active. Electroactive impurities can

Table 6-1. Measured Rate of Cadmium Reduction and Contamination from Solution (from Delahay (3) by permission of Société de Chimie Physique); Cd(II)/Cd(Hg) in 1M K_2SO_4, $0^\circ C$

Time of contact of Electrode and Solution	Measured Rate Constant
(minutes)	(cm. sec. $^{-1}$)
0 (d.m.e., extrapolated)	ca. 0.2
20 (hanging drop)	0.037
40 (hanging drop)	0.016
80 (hanging drop)	0.0065
120 (hanging drop)	0.0038

progressively contaminate a surface as electrolysis proceeds, for instance, if a metal is plated out and thereby changes the nature of the surface. Pre-electrolysis of solutions with an auxiliary electrode is a standard method for removal of electroactive contaminants.

Surface-active contaminants are removed by exposure of the solution to adsorbents — large auxiliary electrodes have been used, but the generally accepted method nowadays is to pass solutions over activated charcoal. The charcoal itself has to be purified before use, the treatment varying according to the source and quality of the charcoal.

A criterion for sufficient purity of the solution is that the observed results do not vary with time of exposure of the electrode to the solution: while the overall reproducibility of experiments depends also on the nature of the electrode surface itself, a time-drift during a single experiment indicates a change in the nature of the surface as a result of exposure to the solution, i.e. resulting from substances present in the solution.

The crystalline nature of the surface is of importance in view of reports that, for a given material, the results depend on the particular crystallographic plane that is exposed to the solution. In addition, some orientations may not be amenable to study — with pyrolytic graphite, for example, solution can penetrate between the "sheets" of graphite if the latter are not parallel to the interface.

The microscopic geometry is important. First of all, the actual surface-area depends on whether the surface is smooth, or whether ridges and valleys are present; thus the apparent, macroscopically measured, area can differ greatly from the true one. Attempts are often made to measure the true surface-area, for instance by measuring the amount of adsorption of a gas on the electrode and calculating the area by use of an adsorption isotherm (most commonly the Brunauer-Emmett-Teller [BET] equation); the validity of this procedure rests on the assumption that the surface available for adsorption of small molecules from the gas phase is identical with that available to substances in solution, the latter substances often being much larger molecules. Another common procedure is to measure the double-layer capacity, assume some value for the correct double-layer capacity per unit area, and hence calculate the area; although frequently used, this procedure is at least as fallible as the first, in view of problems connected with capacity measurements at solid electrodes (see Sections 6.3, 7.3.5).

Further, irregularities such as sharp projections influence the distribution of potential at the interface, and thus can result in some sites being electroactive at an *average* "electrode potential" different from the local potential at which some electrode process actually occurs. A consequence of differences of potential at various places on the surface is that the overall observed processes appear to occur at less sharply defined potentials, since the latter are average potentials; thus, adsorption-desorption (tensammetric) waves at solid electrodes are frequently broader than at mercury. Corrosion processes are also often associated with variations of local potential; some sites act as anodes and others as cathodes, leading to local currents and dissolution (corrosion) of the surface at particular places, and often without the flow of net current through the external circuit (if any). Attempts to prepare smooth surfaces by mechanical polishing are acknowledged to be of doubtful reliability when smoothness at the level of molecular dimensions is sought; better approaches seem to be melting and subsequent solidification (although crystallization may then occur) and/or electrochemical polishing.

Finally, the *actual* macroscopic geometry is important; what is ostensibly a plane-disc electrode may actually be the outside of a closed cylinder if the edges of the disc are not completely sealed and insulated. Quite small imperfections of this sort can profoundly alter the observed phenomena.

The factors mentioned refer to characterization of the surface in a physical sense. The chemical nature of the surface is also frequently not what it may seem to be. Metals and some types of graphite usually are covered by surface films containing oxygen, be it physically adsorbed, chemisorbed, or as a compound with the electrode material. Such films must be removed, unless of course one specifically wishes to examine their properties. Removal of oxygen-containing films can often be carried out by electrolytic reduction. Alternatively, the electrodes can be prepared in an inert atmosphere.

A useful technique for detecting surface-oxide films is cyclic voltammetry. Current is measured while the potential is swept cathodically and then anodically (or *vice versa*), the range of potential excursions and the rate of potential change being variable and controllable. Often, the first cathodic sweep shows a higher cathodic current than subsequent sweeps (Fig. 6-1), indicating reduction of a layer (presumably oxygen-containing) present on the electrode when it is first exposed to the solution. This higher current can frequently be observed again if the potential is taken to a suf-

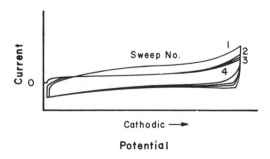

Fig. 6-1. Cyclic voltammogram showing larger cathodic current on first sweep than on repetition, indicative of initially present anodic film. Obtained at Pt electrode, but typical of behavior at many electrode materials.

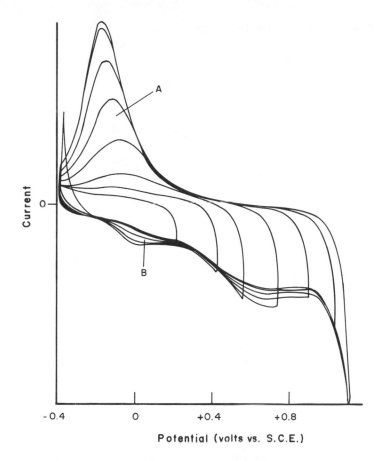

Fig. 6-2. Film formation at Pt (1M KF, aqueous, oxygen-free). At potentials anodic to 0.4V, an anodic film is formed which on cathodic sweep, is reduced (peak A), Peak B appears as A increases, and indicates another anodic process.

ficiently anodic potential, indicating an anodic process that regenerates the film (Fig. 6-2). Such experiments are of value in determining the range of potentials over which a particular electrode can usefully be employed as an "inert" electrode, as well as for studying the process of anodic-film formation and dissolution. The latter are not only of inherent interest and importance, but are also of concern in relation to the passivation of metals, where formation of oxygen-containing layers has been correlated with the onset of passivation (cessation of dissolution of the metal).

It can be seen that work with solid electrodes requires careful and systematic experimentation if the nature of the electrode being used is to be properly defined and understood. The problems are multiplied when one seeks reproducibility, since a method must be evolved for the preparation of identical surfaces. Thus, mechanical polishing is a frequently used procedure, but entails uncertainties in the degree of smoothness achieved (and hence the true surface-area); moreover, polishing may fracture the insulated covering. With all these factors involved, it is not surprising that comparatively little precise and reproducible data is available for solid electrodes as compared to that accumulated in studies on mercury.

103

6.3   Double-Layer Measurements at Solid Electrodes

The methods that have been successful at mercury electrodes have not been success-fully applied at solid electrodes.

The measurement of surface tension at a liquid metal electrode meets no insuperable experimental difficulties. However, there is no accepted method for determining the surface tension between a solid electrode and an electrolyte solution; several methods have been proposed and tried, but insufficient work has been done with these to establish whether the measured quantity — hardness, frictional coefficient, exten-sibility, contact angle of a bubble — is actually a reliable measure of the surface tension. References to such work are given in a recent review (4) and a monograph (5).

The second technique that has been widely used at mercury electrodes is measure-ment of the differential capacity. This method has failed in almost every case when applied to solid electrodes (however, some recent measurements appear to have been successful (6)). If the measurement is valid, the capacity values obtained should be independent of the frequency of the electrical signal used in making the measure-ments. To an excellent approximation, this has been found to be true with spherical mercury electrodes over a wide range of frequencies (from less than 100 Hz to sev-eral tens of kilohertz). On the other hand, it is normally found with solid electrodes that the measured capacity varies, and very appreciably, with the frequency of the signal — behavior termed *"frequency dispersion"*of the capacity. A number of rea-sons for frequency dispersion have been identified and/or suggested:* penetration of electrolyte solution between the electrode and its insulation or mount, inhomo-geneity of the electrode surface, the presence of contaminants on the surface, the presence of films (such as oxides) on the surface, asymmetrical arrangement of the electrode and the counter electrode. There have been one or two papers (7) indicat-ing that measurements at spherical solid electrodes may show only a small frequency dispersion when environmental conditions, especially purity, are very carefully con-trolled; however, the fact is that there is at present no appreciable body of reliable data bearing on the structure of the electrical double-layer at solid electrodes, and our understanding in this area comes almost exclusively from experiments carried out at liquid metals, virtually all of it at mercury (although some results have been ob-tained at liquid gallium).

6.4   Faradaic Studies at Solid Electrodes

From the viewpoint of experimental difficulties, studies of faradaic processes at solid electrodes fall into two distinct categories. If the overall electrochemical pro-cess is controlled in rate by mass transport, then reproducible experimentation is relatively easy since the magnitude of the current is determined by the projected macroscopic area of the electrode and is insensitive to the nature of the surface itself or to slight contamination. On the other hand, if the rate of charge transfer

---

* Frequency dispersion of the capacity is discussed further in Section 7.3.5

(or some other heterogenous reaction) is controlling, then the system is likely to be extremely sensitive to everything that affects the nature of the surface.

Consequently, a number of analytical techniques successfully employ solid electrodes; the application of rotating discs and ring-disc electrodes has been mentioned in Chapter 4. On the other hand, few values of charge-transfer rate-constants at solid electrodes have been reported.

When a substance is deposited at a solid electrode, the surface is permanently altered (except when the product is a gas that is subsequently released). In the electrolytic deposition of metals, the way in which freshly deposited material fits into the existing crystal lattice has an important bearing on the character of the electrochemical process. Thus, there are a number of non-equivalent sites at which charge transfer may take place. A cation may be discharged on a plane, or at the intersection of two planes, in a corner where three planes intersect, or at vacancies in a plane or at an edge (Fig. 6-3); the energetics of the reaction depends on which type of site is involved since the degree of desolvation required, and the degree to which lattice energy is released, are influenced by this factor.

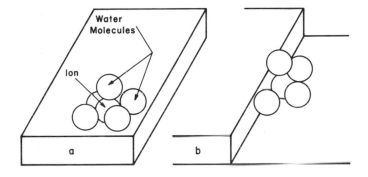

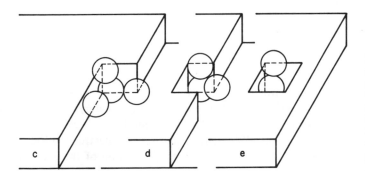

Fig. 6-3. Diagrammatic representation of possible modes of hydration of transferred adions at various sites upon the metal surface; from Conway and Bockris (8) (reproduced by permission of Royal Society).

105

The site at which charge transfer takes place and the site at which the atom is incorporated into the electrode lattice are not necessarily the same. The cation may first be adsorbed on the surface *(adion)*; the adion may be discharged either at the point where it is first adsorbed, or at some other place after moving across the surface. After discharge, we have an atom adsorbed on the surface *(adatom)*, and the adatom may be incorporated in the lattice at the point of discharge, or at some other place after movement across the surface. The sequence of events depends on the relative rates at which adions can be discharged at different possible sites, and the rates at which adatoms can be incorporated into the lattice at different sites. Which of these steps (or some other) is rate-determining also depends on other conditions such as the prevailing current-density — one mechanism may prevail at low current-density, to be replaced by another mechanism at high current-densities. Factors that determine the mechanism include the number of active growth-sites (which may depend on the potential or on the current-density), the fact that the mean distance of movement of adions and adatoms decreases as the number of discharge and growth sites increases, inhomogeneity of current density at different points on the surface, and so on.

In the growth of electro-deposits, a number of different types of deposits are observed. Growth may occur in the form of dendrites (as for instance the crystalline structure of snowflakes), or the surface may grow in pyramids, layers, blocks, ridges, spirals, whiskers, and combinations of these. In addition to the factors mentioned earlier, one needs to be aware that electrocrystallization processes are influenced in very specific and marked ways by the presence of very small amounts of impurities that may inhibit one or other step in the overall processes. At mercury electrodes, inhibition processes are relatively uncomplicated in that one can explain the behavior in terms of the degree of coverage of the surface without taking into account different types of sites on the surface that may be affected. By contrast, inhibition at solid electrodes may occur by the blocking of one type of site, leading to deposition by an entirely different mechanism. A general descriptive account of the important features of electrocrystallization processes has been given by Bockris and Razumney (9).

Clearly, mechanisms and rates of electrochemical reactions at solid surfaces depend on many factors that are not encountered at liquid electrodes. While a great deal of work has been done, there are considerable gaps in our understanding and the generalizations that can safely be drawn are few.

6.5   Electrocatalysis

It has been mentioned that solid electrodes frequently show specific chemical effects in faradaic reactions; such effects can be described operationally as catalytic, since the rate of the overall process is usually influenced considerably by such effects. Particularly in reactions relevant to fuel cells, where a high rate of electrochemical transformation is sought, much work has been devoted to elucidation of the catalytic properties of electrodes. This type of study has come to be called "electrocatalysis". While that term is descriptive of one facet of such investigations, however, it is well to remember that only a complete analysis of the mechanism of a faradaic process will permit understanding of the nature of the catalytic effect.

In the electrolytic oxidation of hydrocarbons, one of the steps is frequently the dissociation of the hydrocarbon through formation of metal-hydrogen bonds. Thus, metals that promote such dissociation (e.g., platinum) have electrocatalytic activity in the oxidation of hydrocarbons. However, for the overall process of oxidation it appears that the presence of oxygen at the surface is also required, and there are thus opposing requirements that (a) the surface be free of oxygen to promote formation of metal-hydrogen bonds but (b) the surface should be at least partly covered with oxygen to promote reaction steps subsequent to the dissociation. This situation has prompted the search for electrocatalysts that simultaneously hold oxygen and also promote electrode-hydrogen bond-formation; electrodes of mixed composition represent one possible solution that is being studied. A possible alternative is a "pulsed" reaction in which dissociation proceeds at a cathodically polarized (oxygen-free) electrode, followed by an anodic pulse to produce oxidation.

The extent to which specific effects of the electrode material can influence the rates of faradaic processes is illustrated (10) by the fact that the rate constant for the hydrogen-evolution reaction varies by a factor of 10^{10} at different metals; for the oxygen-evolution reaction, by a factor of 10^5. For hydrogen evolution, the rate at zone-refined iron is an order of magnitude smaller than at iron containing 0.1% carbon.

Specific effects of the electrode material have also been reported in work on the electrochemical synthesis of organic compounds. For example, in the reduction of ketones, some electrodes lead primarily to production of hydrocarbons whereas others (generally those showing large hydrogen overvoltages) favor production of pinacols (11). The reasons for such effects remain to be elucidated by systematic study of the reaction mechanisms. It may also be that some of the reported effects are not entirely due to specific chemical effects, since it has also been reported that the reaction product may be different at a given electrode, depending on whether the electrode is rotated or remains stationary (12). Moreover, the earlier work on electrosynthesis was carried out without adequate control of the potential of the working electrode; the reported specificity of different materials in determining the nature of the reaction needs to be substantiated by work under controlled-potential conditions.

The term "electrocatalysis" has been used to describe phenomena at mercury electrodes also. Thus, the reduction of In(III) is facilitated by some ligands and this has been called an electrocatalytic effect (13). (It is noteworthy in this particular system that *negative* charge-transfer resistances have been observed, as also previously in other cases (14). That the negative resistance has physical significance is demonstrated by the use of a cell displaying this effect as a negative-resistance element in an oscillator (15)).

Thus, "electrocatalysis" may refer to a range of phenomena, the unifying concept being that of the acceleration of a faradaic process, albeit in an unspecified way.

6.6 Surfactant Effects at Solid Electrodes

It was noted at the outset of this chapter that adsorption generally plays a central role in processes at solid electrodes; a possible exception is the group of analytical methods based on mass-transport control.

Adsorption of non-electroactive surfactants at solid electrodes has been investigated by capacity measurements, and the reported results are qualitatively similar to those described in Chapter 5. Details and references are available in the review by Frumkin and Damaskin (16), and the monographs by Delahay (17) and Damaskin et al. (5).

Effects produced by surfactants on faradaic processes were discussed in Section 5.4 on the basis of results obtained at mercury electrodes. The general comments made there can be expected to be applicable also to processes at solid electrodes. In addition, however, it must be kept in mind that adsorption of the electroactive species is commonly important at solid electrodes, so that there one expects greater sensitivity to the presence of surface-active substances, even in very small amounts.

In the case of electrocrystallization, surfactants exert major effects since the "active" areas of the electrode are generally not the whole area but discrete sites or edges (Section 6.4). Details may be found in the book by Bockris and Razumney (9).

6.7 References

1. D.C.Grahame, *J.Amer. Chem. Soc., 63* (1941) 1207
2. R.N.Adams, *Electrochemistry at Solid Electrodes* (Dekker 1969)
3. P.Delahay, *J. Chim. Phys.*, (1957) 369
4. H.H.Bauer, P.J.Herman and P.J.Elving, *Modern Aspects of Electrochemistry* (in press)
5. B.B. Damaskin, O.A. Petrii and V.V. Batrakov, *Adsorption of Organic Compounds on Electrodes* (Plenum Press 1971)
6. M.Rosen, D.R.Flinn and S.Schuldiner, *J.Electrochem. Soc., 116* (1969) 1112; J-P.Randin and E.Yeager, *J.Electrochem. Soc., 118* (1971) 711
7. D.C.Grahame, R.E.Ireland and R.C.Petersen, *Tech. Rept. no. 22* (1956) *ONR Contract N8-onr-66903*
8. B.E.Conway and J. O'M.Bockris, *Proc. Roy. Soc. London, A248* (1958) 394
9. J.O'M.Bockris and G.Razumney, *Fundamental Aspects of Electrocrystallization* (Plenum Press 1967)
10. J.O'M. Bockris and H.Wroblowa, *Electrochemical Catalysis*, AGA R-Dograph no. 81 (1964) 717-767; *Chem. Abstr. 69*: 48615f
11. M.J.Allen, **Organic Electrode Processes** (Reinhold 1958)
12. H.V.K.Udupa and B.B.Dey, *Proc. 6th Mtg. CITCE, Poitiers 1954* (Butterworths) p. 87
13. R. de Levie and A.A.Husovsky, *J.Electroanal. Chem., 22* (1969) 29
14. H.H.Bauer, *J.Electroanal. Chem., 12* (1966) 64
15. R.Tamamushi, *J.Electroanal. Chem., 11* (1966) 65
16. A.N.Frumkin and B.B.Damaskin, *Modern Aspects of Electrochemistry no. 3* (1964) 149
17. P.Delahay, *Double Layer and Electrode Kinetics* (Interscience 1965) Chapter 6

Electrochemical Measurements

7.1 Introductory

It is not intended to attempt here a survey of electrochemical methodology. Rather, the intention is to mention some points that are often neglected or inadequately treated, and others that are discussed only in comparatively recent literature and have not yet been treated in comprehensive reviews or in books. Attention will be focused on measurements relating to the structure of the double layer, control of electrode potential (including the question of liquid-junction potentials), and the application of radioisotopic and optical methods to the study of electrode processes. This choice of topics is also influenced by the aim of putting into some perspective the experimental bases and corollaries of some of the concepts discussed in earlier ' chapters. An excellent comprehensive yet concise review of electrochemical methods has been recently given by Yeager and Kuta (1).

7.2 Electrocapillary Studies

It has been shown (see Chapter 3) that the structure of the electrical double-layer can be studied *via* measurements of surface tension. These measurements can often be accurately made by means of the Lippmann electrometer. In this type of instrument, the solution being investigated makes contact with mercury in a fine capillary; the head of mercury is adjusted (for example, at different electrode potentials) so that the mercury meniscus is always at the same height in the capillary; the pressure of mercury then permits the surface tension to be calculated.

Frequently, the drop time of a dropping mercury electrode is measured as an alternative to the use of an electrometer; the drop time is closely proportional to surface tension (2).

The capillary electrometer has been long regarded as a very precise instrument, permitting surface tension to be determined to within a fraction of a per cent; details regarding the use of the capillary electrometer are available in the literature (3). Recently, however, attention has been drawn to cases where the mercury meniscus appears to stick in the capillary, casting some doubt on measurements made at large polarizations (both positive and negative to the e.c.m.), particularly in dilute solutions of electrolytes (4); where this occurs, the drop-time technique may be more reliable, since results obtained in this way are in better agreement with capacity data (5) (when the latter conflict with results obtained with a capillary electrometer).

Situations where capacity and surface-tension data are not in agreement have been the subject of recent discussions, leading to a re-examination of the reliability of the capillary electrometer. That instrument is used on the assumption that the contact angle between mercury and glass is constant, and that assumption is apparently not always valid — particularly not at low electrolyte concentrations and at high polarizations. The drop-time method is not affected by changes in contact angle; however, the drop time is not *precisely* (though it is closely) proportional to surface tension, and the method is also not suitable when appreciable time is required to reach equilibrium — as, for instance, in the presence of small concentrations of adsorbable species whose adsorption is diffusion-controlled. It now appears that the method of choice for surface-tension studies is the technique of maximum bubble-pressure:

The maximum pressure that can be applied to mercury in a capillary (orifice pointing upwards) before droplets begin to emerge is directly proportional to the surface tension. This maximum pressure always occurs at the same shape of the mercury-solution interface, so that the contact angle is invariant. The pressure can be increased very slowly, so that equilibrium can be achieved. Recent work with this technique has been reported by Schiffrin (6); automation of the method has been carried out by Lawrence and Mohilner (7), who found the method to be precise to at least $\pm$ 0.2 dyne cm^{-1}.

7.3 Capacity of the Double Layer

7.3.1 A. C. Bridge Methods

The general aspects of an impedance bridge are illustrated in Fig. 7-1. Two arms of the bridge (*ab* and *ad*) contain electrical components of fixed values — for instance,

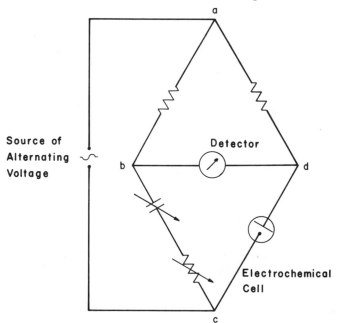

Fig. 7-1. An impedance bridge; details in text.

resistors of equal magnitude. A third arm (cd) contains the electrochemical cell, and the fourth — or measuring — arm (bc) contains electrical components whose values are adjustable. A sinusoidal electrical signal is applied between points a and c, and the potential difference between points b and d is monitored. The bridge is in balance when the potential difference between b and d is zero, i.e., when the ratio of the impedances, bc/(ab+bc), is equal to dc/(ad+dc); in the simplest case, where the impedances of ab and ad are equal, those of bc and cd are also equal at balance.

It has been said the bridge measurements are the most precise ones that can be made, because they involve null-point instead of deflection measurements. However, within the context of electrochemical work, such a statement ignores the fact that it is errors other than those associated with the electrical measurement itself that limit precision. Even comparing bridge measurements with others from a purely electrical point of view (see below), the prospective advantages of accuracy obtainable with bridges may not be realized unless the experimenter is aware of the many possible pitfalls associated with such work.

Electrochemical measurements with impedance bridges involve two factors that are not necessarily involved when bridges are used to determine the characteristics of conventional electrical components. Electrochemists are interested in the impedances at electrodes biased at various potentials by the application of a direct voltage, and this introduces problems not otherwise encountered. Secondly, the alternating voltage used in the measurement should be small — of the order of millivolts — and it is frequently desirable that measurements be carried out over a wide range of frequencies, if possible to frequencies below those of the power line (50 or 60 hertz) and also as high as tens of kilohertz and even higher.

The direct voltage to be applied to the electrochemical cell may be taken from a polarizing circuit that is in series with the a.c. circuit, or by one that is in parallel with the arm of the bridge in which the electrochemical cell is placed. In the first case (Fig. 7-2), the bridge measures the impedance of the electrochemical cell plus that of the d.c. polarizing circuit, which is clearly undesirable; even if the resistance of the d.c. circuit is quite low, the precision of the measurements is adversely affected at higher frequencies, where the (often small — less than 100 ohms) electrolyte resistance of the cell forms the major part of the cell impedance. In view of the small resistances involved, not a great deal can be gained by shunting the d.c. circuit with a capacitor.

Further, the balancing arm (bc) of the bridge must be a parallel rather than a series combination of resistance and capacity so that a path is provided for the flow of direct current. This is inconvenient because a calculation must then be made of the equivalent *series* values of capacity and resistance that would produce balance, since the electrochemical cell simulates such a series combination (in measurements of double-layer capacity in absence of a faradaic process). Therefore, application of the direct voltage by means of a parallel circuit (Fig. 7-3) is the method that has been almost invariably used.

In order that the parallel circuit should not affect the measured impedance of the

111

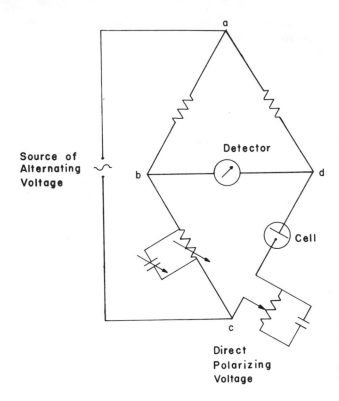

Source of
Alternating
Voltage

Detector

Cell

Direct
Polarizing
Voltage

Fig. 7-2. Impedance bridge
with direct polarizing circuit in series with the
electrochemical cell; rarely
used (see text).

electrochemical cell, it is necessary that the impedance to alternating current of the
parallel circuit be very much higher than that of the electrochemical cell. On the
other hand, the resistance to direct current should not be high. Therefore, one uses
a choke (L, Fig. 7-3) in the d.c. polarizing circuit. This way of carrying out measurements limits the performance of the bridge at low frequencies. Here, the impedance
of the electrochemical cell is determined almost entirely by that of the electrical
double-layer. Typically, the capacity of the double layer is of the order of $1\mu f$
($20\ \mu f/cm^2$ at a microelectrode of area $1/20\ cm^2$); the impedance of the double
layer is therefore $(1/10^{-6}\omega)$ ohms and a choke of the same impedance would have
inductance, L, given by

$$L = \text{impedance}/\omega = 1/10^{-6}\omega^2 \qquad (7\text{-}1)$$

Consequently, at 50 hertz ($\omega = 2\pi f = 314$) such a choke would have an inductance
of about 10 henries. Under these conditions, the measured impedance of the cell
would be considerably less than the correct value, since the parallel arm has the
same impedance. In order that the impedance measurement may reflect the impedance of the cell within one per cent, a choke is required whose magnitude is approximately one hundred times that of the cell; in the present case, this would
require a choke of 1000 henries inductance (these calculations assume that the phase
shift is the same in the cell and in the parallel circuit — thus, only a guide to the
order of magnitude is given here). Chokes of this magnitude, where available, inev-

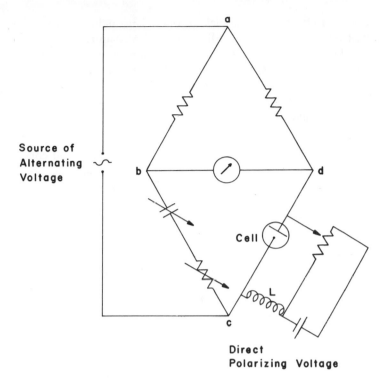

Cell

L

Direct
Polarizing Voltage

Fig. 7-3. Impedance bridge with direct polarizing circuit parallel with bridge circuit; frequency
limits discussed in text.

itably have distributed capacity of sufficient magnitude that the choke behaves not
as an inductor (whose impedance increase linearly with increasing frequency) but as
a tuned circuit of inductance and capacity in parallel, with a maximum impedance
at a certain resonance frequency and a lower impedance both at higher frequencies
and at lower frequencies. Therefore, in order to carry out measurements at fairly
low frequencies, it is necessary to examine carefully the characteristics of the choke
used, and perhaps to deliberately add capacity in parallel in order to bring the resonance frequency to the desired value; furthermore, it is then necessary to change
this capacity as the measuring frequency is changed (8) and it may also be necessary
to use different inductors in different ranges of frequency.

In practice, very little work has been reported with such arrangements at frequencies
below a few hundred hertz. At frequencies of several hundred hertz and higher,
conveniently available chokes of a hundred henries or less can be successfully used.

The need to work with alternating voltages of small magnitude means that noise has
to be kept to a small value. The bridge and all electrochemical components need
to be electrostatically shielded, and care taken that the shields and the ground connections on the instruments be grounded in such a way as to avoid ground loops.
Because of the difficulty of shielding a dropping-mercury-electrode assembly, it is
convenient to make this point in the circuit a grounded point when possible. It may

113

also be necessary to eliminate electromagnetic pickup; where large inductors are used, these are best shielded in mumetal cases. Elimination of pick-up can be facilitated if one remembers that the removal of sources of radiation can be even more helpful than attempting to shield these from the places where pick-up may occur. Leads to the power mains, and power transformers, should be kept as far as possible from the bridge and the electrochemical cell. The direction in which power transformers face can be important.

The grounding of shields and the avoidance of ground loops calls for a certain amount of care. Ground loops result from the fact that all so-called ground points and connections are not necessarily precisely at ground potential, nor even at the same potential. This situation can be minimized by using wires of large cross-section to make all ground connections, but it is not generally possible to eliminate the effect altogether. When a connection is made between two "ground" points that differ somewhat in potential, and from each of these to some part of the circuit, current will flow in the resulting loop. In the case of bridge measurements, a false balance-point can result from the presence of ground loops. Care must always be taken, therefore, to connect the circuit to ground at only a single point; where electronic instruments are used with three-pin connections (of which one is to a ground point) it is usually best to use adaptors so that the instruments are not grounded at the mains supply, but only at the input side of the instruments. The connection to ground is best made by a separate lead; often, cold-water pipes suffice for this purpose.

It is also important to realize that ground loops can be set up even when there are no wires actually completing the loop. Alternating signals can be transmitted from one part of the circuit to another if these are coupled together capacitively. For example, in transformers with grounded shields it is common to find that alternating current can flow from the coil to ground because of the capacity present between these points. Capacitive coupling is also present when shielded cables are used, and it is helpful if the latter have relatively thick plastic dielectric, giving a low capacity per unit length of cable.

Various types of bridges have been described in connection with electrochemical work. Reference to the literature concerned with electrical measurements *per se*, however, shows that electrochemists have not necessarily made the best use of available knowledge in this area. It is most desirable that workers entering this field should familiarize themselves with the principles of electrical measurements (see, for example, Buckingham and Price (9)). The presence of ground loops is particularly likely in the case of electrochemical measurements because of the physical size and nature of the electrochemical cell and the associated reference electrodes and salt bridges. It is therefore rather surprising that in many cases no attention appears to have been paid to this possibility, although there is a standard electrical method ("Wagner earth") of avoiding a false balance from this cause.

Furthermore, bridges may contain any combination of electrical components in the ratio arms (*ab* and *ad* in Fig. 7-1), yet often it seems that electrochemists have not chosen the type of bridge best suited to their purpose. As a general rule, pick-up of stray radiation occurs to an extent that is determined by the impedance of the component in which pick-up occurs. Consequently, it is convenient where possible to use circuits of low impedance. The use of transformer-ratio bridges (10) then becomes attractive; little attention has yet been given to these in electrochemical work, however.

Hills and Payne (11) have given a very useful and comprehensive discussion of the use of bridges in electrochemical measurements.

7.3.2 A.C. Polarography

The impedance characteristics of an electrochemical cell can be determined by measuring the alternating current through the cell as a function of the alternating voltage across it (or vice versa) and the phase shift between the current and voltage. This contrasts with measurements with a bridge, where both the magnitude and phase of the impedance are obtained directly from the magnitudes of the capacity and resistance required to achieve balance. The bridge technique, however, is less convenient experimentally since the variable capacity and resistance must be adjusted alternately, a number of times, in order to achieve balance; this is made particularly laborious when a dropping mercury electrode is used, since balance must be achieved at a known time in the life of the drop, and this necessitates the use of an additional timing device and subsequent correction of resistance and capacity values in order to relate them to a single time in the life of a drop (i.e., to a constant area of the electrode). By contrast, a single measurement of the magnitude of the impedance and a single measurement of the phase shift can be carried out in less time than is required to balance a bridge.

The magnitude of the impedance of the cell can be obtained in a number of ways: a predetermined alternating voltage can be applied and the alternating current in the circuit measured (a.c. polarography (12)); or an alternating current of known magnitude may be caused to flow through the cell and the resulting voltage measured (8); in either of these modes a substitution method may be used in which, for each measurement, the cell is replaced by a variable resistor and the latter adjusted so that the current- (or potential-) measuring device shows the same deflection as when the electrochemical cell is in the circuit. Such a substitution method normally makes possible a higher accuracy since the results obtained do not depend on the linearity of response of amplifiers or meters, being in this sense a null method.

The phase shift can be measured in a number of ways. The alternating current and voltage can be displayed in X-Y form on the screen of an oscilloscope and the phase angle calculated from the shape of the figure obtained. Alternatively, a phase shifter can be incorporated in the circuit and the signal from the phase shifter, together with the voltage across the cell, displayed on an oscilloscope; the phase shift can be altered by varying the magnitudes of the components of the phase shifter until the oscilloscope shows a straight line — then, the phase shift can be calculated from the values of the components of the phase shifter at that point. One can also obtain commercially phase-meters that indicate either in analogue or in digital form the phase shift between two components. These instruments frequently can also be used as phase-selective voltmeters, enabling the in-phase and out-of-phase magnitudes of voltages to be measured; then, one can use these two measurements to completely describe the impedance characteristics of the electrochemical cell.

An experimental convenience of methods using meters is that the presence of ground loops is immediately apparent. If the applied alternating voltage (or current) is set to zero, the current- (or voltage-) measuring instrument should also show zero; if this is not the case, the presence of a ground loop (or of stray pick-up) is indicated.

A.C. polarography lends itself to automation: instruments have been described (13, 14) that provide read-out and recording of in-phase and out-of-phase signals, and this methodology appears attractive for double-layer-capacity measurements. However, the available frequency range is not usually large with these instruments; where it is necessary or desirable to work over a wide frequency range, well-established manual methodology is available (15).

7.3.3 Charging Curves

When a constant current is applied to a series combination of a resistance and a capacity, the potential across this combination changes with time as shown in Fig. 7-4.

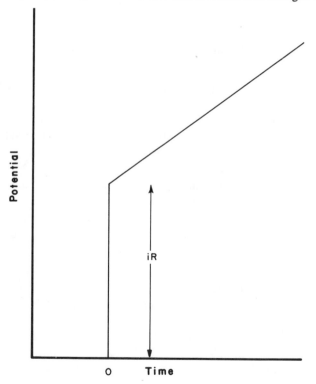

Fig. 7-4. Potential-*vs.*-time function when constant current i is applied at t=0 to series combination of resistance R and capacity C.

The potential can be expressed in terms of the magnitudes of the resistance, R, and of the capacity, C, in the form

$$E = iR + it/C \qquad (7-2)$$

where t is the time after application of the current, i. Clearly, the resistance can be calculated from the magnitude of the potential that is obtained instantaneously upon application of the current, and the magnitude of the capacity can be calculated from the rate at which the potential increases with time after application of the current. This method has been quite widely used, especially in connection with capacity measurements at solid electrodes, sometimes by the use of a fixed current and at other times by the use of a current that is of square-wave form. In the latter case, the potential varies with time as shown in Fig. 7-5, and interpretation is similar to that just described.

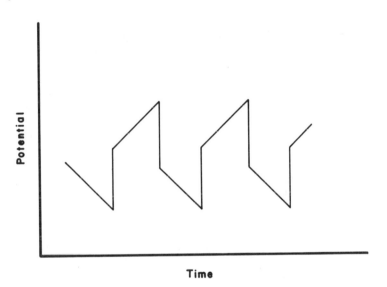

Fig. 7-5. Potential-*vs.*-time function when square-wave current is applied to series combination of resistance and capacity.

The disadvantage of such a technique in electrochemical work is that one must assume *a priori* that the cell does in fact simulate the behavior of a resistance and a capacity in series. If such an equivalent circuit is not valid, the potential will change with time in a way that differs from those shown in Fig. 7-4 and 7-5. However, small discrepancies are not readily detectable with such a method of measurement. For the particular case (often encountered) where the apparent capacity is a function of frequency, the variation of potential with time is non-linear instead of linear. However, the degree of non-linearity is not accurately measurable when, as is usual, one observes oscilloscope tracings, and the fit of the series-resistance-and-capacity model cannot be judged as readily with this technique as with one that employs variable-frequency sinusoidal signals.

117

7.3.4 Pulse and Step Techniques

The technique of charging curves is one example of the application of a step function — the current is changed from zero to some chosen value "instantaneously". Similar information (about electrochemical reactions, as well as about the double layer) is obtainable by application of a potential step, or with current or potential pulses, or square waves. Analysis of the results has often been carried out on the assumption that the applied signal is the theoretically desired one. However, in practice there are always imperfections due to the nature of the circuit—finite switching times, rise-times of amplifiers, distributed capacity, and so on. Consequently, each experimental arrangement has some lower time-limit for reliable work, where at shorter times the observed variable is so greatly influenced by the characteristics of the electrical circuit that information about the electrode process cannot be extracted.

This time-limit can be shortened if one measures not only the dependent variable (current, say) but also the applied signal (voltage, say). In that case one does not restrict the useful time-scale to that determined by, e.g., rise time but to the shorter interval during which the two signals reach a measurable value. This idea has been discussed and implemented by Pilla (16), who has succeeded in making measurements down to about 10 nanoseconds. The data is obtained in terms of impedance at various times, and transformed into a frequency spectrum by computer processing. This technique combines the advantages of conventional impedance studies with the minimal time requirements of pulse techniques. It appears to be a considerable advance in methodology, and should be ideal for studies in which the nature of the surface changes with time, e.g. at solid electrodes where film formation and electrocrystallization occur. One can obtain a complete frequency spectrum at intervals of seconds (or less if required), and observe how the processes change as the character of the surface changes.

7.3.5 Frequency Dispersion

Variation of the measured double-layer capacity with frequency of the measuring signal is often observed, particularly with solid electrodes. Many causes have been postulated to account for the dispersion (17), and no doubt different explanations are valid in different cases; some generalizations can, however, be made.

It is worth noting that the equivalent circuit of a single resistance in series with a single capacity can hold only if the distribution of current between the working electrode and the counter electrode is uniform, i.e. when the current density is the same at all points on the working electrode. When this is not the case, the equivalent circuit consists of a number of parallel paths (see Fig. 7-6). The impedance of each path is given by

$$Z_i = R_i - j/\omega C_i \tag{7-3}$$

and the impedance of the network as a whole is given by

$$\frac{1}{Z} = \Sigma \frac{1}{Z_i} = \Sigma \frac{1}{R_i - j/\omega C_i} \tag{7-4}$$

118

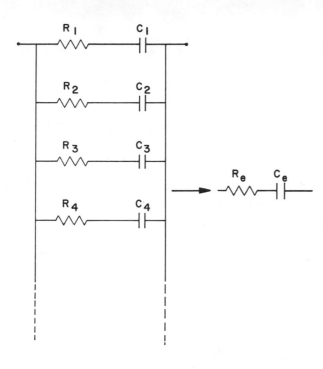

Fig. 7-6. Representation of the circuit on the left by that on the right leads to values of R_e and C_e that vary with frequency. See text for application to double-layer studies.

$$= \Sigma \frac{R_i + j/\omega C_i}{R_i^2 + 1/\omega^2 C_i^2} \tag{7-5}$$

If the total impedance is to be represented by a single resistance, R_E, in series with a single capacity, C_E, one has

$$\frac{1}{Z} = \frac{1}{R_E - j/\omega C_E} = \frac{R_E + j/\omega C_E}{R_E^2 + 1/\omega^2 C_E^2} \tag{7-6}$$

so that (equating real and imaginary parts of equations (7-5) and (7-6))

$$R_E/(R_E^2 + 1/\omega^2 C_E^2) = \Sigma \left(R_i / (R_i^2 + 1/\omega^2 C_i^2) \right) \tag{7-7}$$

and

$$1/C_E/(R_E^2 + 1/\omega^2 C_E^2) = \Sigma \left(1/C_i/ (R_i^2 + 1/\omega^2 C_i^2) \right) \tag{7-8}$$

Clearly, the equivalent resistance and capacity vary with frequency; they do not represent the capacity of the electrical double-layer and the resistance of the electrolyte solution. Limiting cases of some interest are those at low and at high frequencies. At very high frequencies,

$$\frac{1}{R_{E(\omega \to \infty)}} = \Sigma \frac{1}{R_i} \tag{7-9}$$

which is to be expected since the capacitive part of the impedance becomes negligible; but

119

$$C_E(\omega \to \infty) = R_E^2(\omega \to \infty) \; \Sigma \; \frac{1}{C_i R_i^2}$$

$$= (\Sigma \; \frac{1}{R_i})^2 \Big/ \Sigma \; \frac{1}{C_i R_i^2} \tag{7-10}$$

which shows that the high-frequency limit is *not* a measure of the "true" double-layer capacity.

At low frequencies, however

$$C_E(\omega \to o) = \Sigma C_i \tag{7-11}$$

which one might term the "true" double-layer capacity; but

$$R_E(\omega \to o) = (\Sigma R_i C_i^2)/(\Sigma C_i)^2 \tag{7-12}$$

so that the low-frequency limit of the resistance does not reflect the "true" resistance of the solution.

The calculation shown above is of illustrative value only, since it is there assumed that the cell can be represented by a set of parallel paths consisting of components of fixed values R_i and C_i. This assumption is not permissible for conditions of alternating signals of varying frequency. However, the conclusions regarding the low- and high-frequency limits are valid: for reliable estimation of double-layer capacities, the low-frequency limit of the observed results should be used. Thus, where the working electrode is subject to a non-uniform current-distribution, an extrapolation to low frequencies is necessary to obtain the double-layer capacity. The procedure of extrapolating to infinite frequency has sometimes been used where the electrode surface was thought to be rough (for references and discussion of this point, see a recent review (17)); equation (7-10) demonstrates that such a procedure is invalid.

A non-uniform current-distribution can arise from a number of different causes. With a dropping mercury electrode, there are two factors that can lead to a frequency dispersion of the double-layer capacity. If a conventional capillary is used, the top of the drop is "shaded" by the presence of the glass of the capillary; it has been shown that the use of fine-tipped capillaries (where this shading is minimized) can lead to a much better constancy of the measured capacity with frequency. The second factor that has been identified as a cause of frequency dispersion is the fact that solution penetrates into the bore of the capillary to varying degrees; this is a clear example of different paths for the alternating current to different parts of the surface, and a very large change with frequency can be obtained even with apparently slight penetration of solution. This penetration has been minimized or overcome by the use of capillaries whose bore is tapered to some extent, and more commonly by treating the bore with silicone compounds to make it water-repellent.

With solid electrodes, penetration can also be present between the electrode material and its insulation or mount; and a non-uniformity of the surface itself can lead to frequency dispersion. In addition, however, the macroscopic geometry of the working electrode is important. Frequency dispersion at the dropping mercury electrode is found in limited frequency ranges, due to "shading" and "solution penetration", but the distribution of current is uniform over the major part of the electrode surface. With electrodes that are not spherical, the degree of non-uniformity of the current distribution can be much greater, and work with solid electrodes has usually involved non-spherical electrodes. Therefore, one could expect to find frequency dispersion at solid electrodes (or at, for instance, mercury-pool electrodes) purely as a result of the macroscopic electrode geometry. The importance of this factor was recently emphasised (17, 18). A theoretical study has been published (19) for a disc electrode surrounded by an insulating plane, and for a drop tangent to an insulating plane. For the disc, there is comparatively little frequency dispersion of the electrolyte resistance but a large effect on the capacity; at the drop, the capacity is comparatively little affected but the resistance is more strongly affected.

It is now clear, therefore, that in attempts to measure double-layer capacities one must consider electrode geometry as well as problems of solution penetration, accumulation of impurities, and so on. Randin and Yeager (20) have recently succeeded in obtaining frequency-independent capacity values at a pyrolytic graphite disc using an electrode fitted with a mask that produces a uniform distribution of current at the electrode. Implementation of this idea, coupled with the careful attention to purity, could lead to considerable progress in studies at solid electrodes.

7.4 Potential of the Indicator Electrode

7.4.1 Liquid-Junction Potentials

At the junction between any two dissimilar electrolyte solutions, a difference of electrical potential arises, the so-called liquid-junction potential. This arises because of the different tendencies to diffuse on the part of the various ions present at various concentrations. The theory of liquid-junction potentials has been examined in some detail (21). The essential points for the present purpose are that there is no way of completely eliminating a liquid-junction potential; and that *a priori* calculation of liquid-junction potentials requires a knowledge of the acitivity coefficients of the individual ions involved; this information is not available, and consequently there remains an uncertainty about electrode potentials whenever solutions of dissimilar electrolytes are in contact. Approximate calculations can be made, and some typical results are shown in Table 7-1. It can be seen that these potentials can vary from very small and perhaps negligible to very appreciable proportions. In general, liquid-junction potentials are small when one of the solutions, present at high concentrations, contains anions and cations whose transport numbers are very closely the same — for instance, in potassium-chloride solutions.

From the point of view of practice, it is important to remember that liquid-junction potentials cannot be calculated or estimated by ascribing fixed contributions to various salt solutions. Thus, the liquid-junction potential between solutions A and B is not the same as the total of all the liquid-junction potentials in a series combination where A is in contact with D and D is in contact with B. An example of

Table 7-1 Estimated Liquid-Junction Potentials (25°C) (from Meites (22) by permission of McGraw-Hill)

Electrolyte (1)	Electrolyte (2)	
	0.1F KCl	3.5F KCl
0.01F HCl	9.3 mV	1.4 mV
0.1F HCl	26.8	3.1
1F HCl	56.2	16.6
0.01F KCl	0.4	1.0
0.1F KCl	0.0	0.6
1F KCl	–	0.2
0.05F H_2SO_4	25	4
0.5F H_2SO_4	53	14

this lack of additivity is given in Table 7-2. Direct measurement of the difference of potential between a mercurous-sulfate reference-electrode and a saturated calomel electrode gives 407-414 mv, a different value from the difference in the half-step potentials of various

Table 7-2 Correction for Liquid-Junction Potentials (data from Tsuji and Elving (23) by permission of American Chemical Society)

Sample Solution	Polarographic Reduction Potential Measured Against			Potentiometric Potential Difference Between the Two Reference Electrodes, Measured	
	Saturated Calomel Electrode (i)	Mercurous Sulfate Electrode (ii)	ΔE (ii)-(i)	Directly	With Interposed Salt Bridge Containing Sample Solution
0.40lmM Tl_2SO_4		1F Na_2SO_4 0.01F H_2SO_4			
0.02F LiCl	-459mV	-849mV	390mV	414.3mV	390.3mV
0.208mM $CdCl_2$		(1F K_2SO_4)			
IF HCl	-642mV	-1083mV	441mV	407.7mV	440.0mV

reduction processes measured against these two reference cells respectively. However, if the difference of potentials between the two reference half-cells is measured using, as a salt bridge between the two electrodes, a solution of the same composition as used in the polarographic work, it turns out that the measured potential differences are, within experimental error, the same as the differences in half-step potentials measured in the two sets of polarographic experiments. This fact should be kept in mind when one seeks to compare half-step potentials obtained with two different reference electrodes, as is frequently necessary.

In considerations dealing with the electrical double-layer, the presence of liquid-junction potentials of unknown magnitude is important, for instance, when one seeks to draw conclusions about the differences of the potential of zero charge in different solutions. These differences are measurable only as magnitudes that include not only the potentials of zero charge, but also the liquid-junction potentials.

Detailed discussions of liquid-junction potentials are available in a number of texts (24).

7.4.2 Three-Electrode Circuits

In any electrical cell containing a working electrode and a reference electrode, the potential of the working electrode relative to the reference is related to the potential applied from the external polarizing circuit by the relationship

$$E_{working} = E_{applied} - iR \qquad (7\text{-}13)$$

where iR represents the potential drop across the solution due to the fact that the current i is flowing across the resistance R of the electrolyte. In many situations, the magnitude of this iR drop is sufficiently great that corrections for it must be made. Such corrections can be quite laborious and it would be convenient if the effect could be eliminated by experimental means. Moreover, in cases where the success of the experiment depends on the precision with which the electrode potential remains constant, it may not be possible to achieve the desired results unless the potential of the working electrode can be kept constant automatically by a rapidly responding system.

Automatic compensation of iR drop is based on the use of three-electrode circuits. The principle of such a circuit is illustrated in Fig. 7-7.

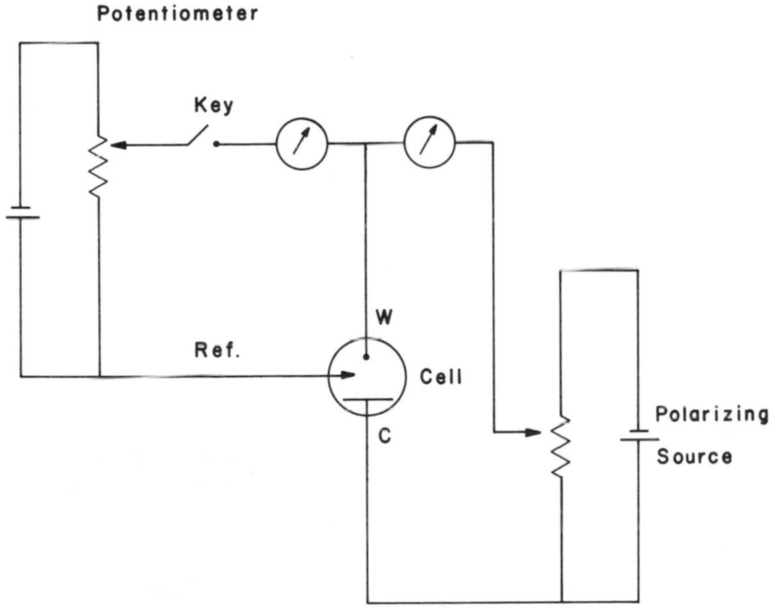

Fig. 7-7. Three-electrode circuit (as in manual polarography).

Current flows between the working electrode W and the counter electrode C and through the external circuit containing in general a source of polarizing voltage and a current-measuring device. One cannot measure the potential of the working electrode by measuring the potential across the whole electrochemical cell because this measurement contains the iR drop. One can, however, introduce a third electrode – a reference – and connect this to the working electrode through a potential-

123

measuring device. If one can arrange that negligible current flows through the reference electrode, then one can measure the potential of the working electrode with respect to the reference electrode without an iR drop (but see below). The measurement can be made in one of two ways: a student-type potentiometer can be used and the potential of the working electrode measured by a null method – at balance, no current flows through the reference electrode; alternatively, one can use a voltmeter of high impedance – e.g. a pH meter – to measure directly the difference of potential between working and reference electrodes; because of the high impedance of the measuring instrument, negligible current is drawn through the reference electrode.

It is important to realize that it is not always possible to eliminate all the iR drop by means of such a three-electrode circuit. For instance, at the dropping mercury electrode most of the electrolyte resistance manifests itself near the electrode, since the lines of current from the (large) counter-electrode converge here and the "column" of solution through which the current flows has its narrowest "cross-section" at the surface of the dropping electrode. Consequently, the electrical potential changes from the surface of the dropping electrode into the solution as a result of iR drop, and exclusion of this potential drop from a measurement is possible only if one can place a reference electrode so close to the surface of the dropping electrode that the iR drop becomes negligible. This "uncompensated" iR drop cannot always be made negligible, e.g. if the conductivity of the solution is low. Then, it becomes necessary to measure the uncompensated resistance and correct for it in calculations, or – in automated instruments – apply positive feedback to compensate for it (13).

Three-electrode circuits as described permit the measurement of the potential of the working electrode with minimum effect from ohmic potential-drop. However, it is sometimes necessary and usually convenient to *maintain* the potential at a desired value. One method of achieving this result involves amplification of the difference between the potential as measured and the desired potential and to use the amplified signal to control a mechanical servo-system that changes the magnitude of the voltage applied from the polarizing source until the actual potential achieved at the working electrode equals the desired value. The response of such a system is inevitably slow because of the mechanical inertia involved. Nowadays, automatic control is achieved by purely electronic means, commonly by use of so-called operational amplifiers. These amplifiers typically have very high gain and can be connected in such a way that the current output depends on the difference of potential applied at two inputs; by making these inputs the desired potential and the actual potential of the working electrode, and feeding the resultant current into the loop containing the working electrode and the counter electrode (see Fig. 7-8), the same result is achieved as by use of a servo system, but the response is very much faster.

The characteristics of operational amplifiers and their application in electrochemical work have been discussed in detail (13, 25); no attempt to cover this subject will be made here, but it should be pointed out that much of the literature treats only the ideal behavior of these amplifiers and of circuits built from them. In practice, operational amplifiers – like any instruments – have practical limitations. With operational amplifiers, it should be remembered that there may be drifts (i.e. the

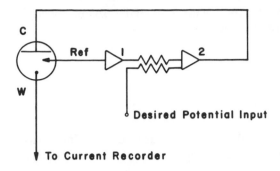

Fig. 7-8. Three-electrode circuit using operational amplifiers. Amplifier 1 is a voltage-follower that prevents the reference electrode from drawing appreciable current. Amplifier 2 (summing amplifier) adjusts its output until the potential difference between the two inputs is zero, i.e. until the potential of the working electrode with respect to the reference electrode is equal to the desired potential difference.

input potential difference is only approximately zero and can change with time); the gain is typically high, but it is nevertheless limited, and one cannot expect iR compensation beyond a certain point; the amplifiers produce noise which may or may not be important in the particular application; grounding and shielding can be vitally important; and because of the high gain, there is a tendency for the amplifiers to go into oscillation. These matters are important even where — as so frequently in the literature — they are left implicit and not explicitly discussed.

7.5 Experiments using Radioactive Tracers

Purely electrical measurements on electrochemical systems are not always capable of providing direct information about some of the phenomena that occur in the cell. For instance, the amounts of certain species adsorbed at the electrode surface can usually be calculated only indirectly from electrical measurements, and often this involves the use of a physical model for the electrochemical process, a model that may or may not be precisely valid. Therefore, considerable attention has been given to the possibility of measuring directly the amounts of adsorbed species at electrodes. One approach to this has been through the use of radioactively tagged adsorbate species, with subsequent measurement of the radioactivity of the molecules attached to the surface of the electrode (26).

Some such measurements have been made by removing the electrode from the solution and measuring its activity. The disadvantage of such a procedure is that when the electrode is removed, the amount of adsorbed substance may be altered. The extent to which this is the case will, of course, depend on the strength of adsorption; in any case, however, one would wish to determine the extent to which such a method is reliable, and the only way of achieving this is to make measurements while the electrode is still immersed in the solution.

Measurements of the amount of adsorption of radioactive species at electrodes immersed in a solution have been made by using electrodes that are at the same time the windows of radiation counters. The problem then is to ensure that the measured radiation comes only from adsorbed molecules, and not from radioactive molecules in the solution in the vicinity of the electrode. To achieve this, cells are used whose

125

cross-section is very narrow near the electrode, with most of the solution being present in reservoirs on either side of the electrode; in this way, radiation is counted only from the electrode and a very thin layer of solution immediately adjacent to it (27, 28).

7.6   Optical Studies of Electrode Surfaces

Since the optical properties of the surface of an electrode depend on the materials on the surface, observation of adsorbed species by optical techniques is in principle possible.

One approach that has been used is the technique of ellipsometry (29-33). A beam of polarized light is reflected from the electrode surface, and the change in polarization as a result of reflection is measured. While interpretation of data obtained in this way presents considerable difficulties, information of a highly interesting nature can result. Thus, film formation at nickel and platinum electrodes has been followed by this technique, and the optical properties of the film correlated with the onset of passivation; the thickness of the films, and their nature (chemisorbed oxygen or metallic oxide), can be inferred from ellipsometric studies.

Spectroscopic methods have also been used. When a beam of light is reflected from the walls of an optical wave-guide, intensity losses occur at wave lengths that correspond to the absorption spectrum of species lying outside the wave-guides. By making electrodes that are at the same time optical wave-guides, it becomes possible to study the absorption spectra of adsorbed molecules at electrode surfaces. Early work using these techniques in both the infrared (34) and visible (35) regions of the spectrum has been reported. The technique is often referred to as frustrated-multiple-internal-reflection spectroscopy. The reader should consult the literature for developments in this field since work in these areas is proceeding actively at the present time.

7.7   References

1. E.Yeager and J.Kuta, *Physical Chemistry — An Advanced Treatise* (Academic Press 1970), vol. *IXA (Electrochemistry)*, chapter 4
2. R.G.Barradas and F.M.Kimmerle, *Can. J. Chem.*, *45* (1967) 109
3. For example, L.G.M.Gordon, J.Halpern and B.Conway, *J.Electroanal. Chem.*, *21* (1969) P3
4. J.Lawrence, R.Parsons and R.Payne, *J. Electroanal. Chem.*, *16* (1968) 193
5. R.Parsons, *Rev. Pure Appl. Chem.*, *18* (1968) 91
6. D.J.Schiffrin, *J.Electroanal. Chem.*, *23* (1969) 168
7. J.Lawrence and D.M.Mohilner, *Spring Mtg. Electrochemical Soc., Los Angeles, May 1970;* Extended Abstracts p. 802 (abstract no. 303)
8. H.H.Bauer, *Electrochemistry, Proc. 1st Australian Conf.* (Pergamon 1964) p. 282
9. H.Buckingham and E.M.Price, *Principles of Electrical Measurements* (English Universities Press 1955)
10. G.H.Nancollas and C.A.Vincent, *J.Sci. Instr.*, *40* (1963) 306
11. G.J.Hills and R.Payne, *Trans. Faraday Soc.*, *61* (1965) 316
12. B.Breyer and H.H.Bauer, *Alternating Current Polarography and Tensammetry* (Interscience 1963)
13. D.E.Smith, *Electroanalytical Chemistry*, *1* (1966) 1; *CRC Critical Reviews in Analytical Chemistry*, *2* (1971) no. l.
14. R. de Levie and A.A.Husovsky, *J.Electroanal. Chem.*, *20* (1969) 181
15. D.Britz and H.H.Bauer, *J.Sci. Instr.*, *44* (1967) 843

16. A.A.Pilla, *J.Electrochem. Soc., 117* (1970) 467
17. H.H.Bauer, P.J.Herman and P.J.Elving, *Modern Aspects of Electrochemistry,* in press
18. H.H.Bauer, M.S.Spritzer and P.J.Elving, *J.Electroanal. Chem., 17* (1968) 299
19. J.Newman, *J.Electrochem. Soc., 117* (1970) 198
20. J-P. Randin and E.Yeager, *J.Electrochem. Soc., 118* (1971) 711
21. L.Bass, *Trans. Faraday Soc., 60* (1964) 1914; and references given there
22. L.Meites, *Handbook of Analytical Chemistry* (McGraw-Hill, 1963), pp.5-15
23. K.Tsuji and P.J.Elving, *Anal. Chem., 41* (1969) 216
24. For example, K.J.Vetter, *Electrochemical Kinetics* (Academic Press 1967) p. 45 ff.; W.M.Clark, *Oxidation-Reduction Potentials of Organic Systems* (Williams and Wilkins 1960); R.G.Bates, *Electrometric pH Determinations* (Wiley 1954)
25. Operational Amplifiers Symposium, *Anal. Chem., 35* (1963) 1770
26. N.A.Balashova and V.E.Kazarinov, *Electroanalytical Chemistry, 3* (1969) 135
27. J.A.Kafalas and H.C.Gatos, *Rev. Sci. Instr., 29* (1958) 47
28. K.Schwabe and W.Schwenke, *Electrochim. Acta. 9* (1964) 1003
29. J.P.Hoare, *The Electrochemistry of Oxygen* (Wiley 1968)
30. A.K.N.Reddy, M.A.V.Devanathan and J. O'M.Bockris, *J. Electroanal. Chem. 6* (1963) 61
31. A.K.N.Reddy, M.Genshaw and J. O'M.Bockris, *J.Electroanal. Chem., 8* (1964) 406
32. A.K.N.Reddy, M.G.B.Rao and J.O'M.Bockris, *J.Chem. Phys., 42* (1965) 2246
33. A.K.N.Reddy, M.A.Genshaw and J.O'M. Bockris, *J.Chem. Phys., 48* (1968) 671
34. H.B.Mark and B.S.Pons, *Anal. Chem., 38* (1966) 119
35. W.N.Hansen, T.Kuwana and R.A.Osteryoung, *Anal. Chem., 38* (1966) 1810

Further Reading

The following references can serve for detailed study of the concepts described in this book, as well as of other topics not discussed.

General Texts

J.Koryta, J.Dvorak and V.Bohackova, *Electrochemistry* (Methuen 1970). A short modern textbook treating ionics and electrode processes.

K.J.Vetter, *Electrochemical Kinetics* (Academic 1967). Detailed treatment of kinetics, discussion of many specific systems, sections on corrosion and passivation.

J. O'M.Bockris and A.K.N.Reddy, *Modern Electrochemistry* (Plenum 1970). Discursively written treatise covering ionics (Vol. 1) and electrode reactions (Vol. 2), including corrosion, batteries and fuel cells.

B.E.Conway, *Theory and Principles of Electrode Processes* (Ronald 1965). Electrode processes discussed in an original manner with emphasis on the role of adsorbed reactants and intermediates.

Topics of General Interest, not covered in most texts on electrochemistry in general

G.J.Hills and P.J.Ovenden, *Adv. Electrochem. Electrochemical Eng.*, 4 (1966) 185. Introduction to, and review of, electrochemistry at high pressures.

J.N.Agar, *Adv. Electrochem. Electrochemical Eng.*, 3 (1963) 31. Thermogalvanic cells.

G.Wenglowski, *Modern Aspects Electrochem.*, 5 (1969) 251. Economic significance of electrochemistry in U.S.A.

W.Vielstich, *Fuel Cells* (Wiley 1970).

M.W.Breiter, *Electrochemical Processes in Fuel Cells* (Springer 1969).

M.J.Allen, *Organic Electrode Processes* (Reinhold 1958). Review of literature dealing primarily with electrosynthesis.

M.Fleischmann and D.Pletcher, *Roy. Inst. Chem. Reviews*, 2 (1969) 87. Reaction mechanisms in electrosynthetic studies.

M.M.Baizer and J.P.Petrovich, *Progr. Phys. Org. Chem.*, 7 (1970) 189. Electrosynthesis, emphasis on coupling processes.

H.Gerischer, in *Treatise on Physical Chemistry, Vol. IX A (Electrochemistry)*, Ch. 5. Semiconductor electrodes.

W.Mehl and J.M.Hale, *Adv. Electrochem. Electrochemical Eng.*, 6 (1967) 399. Electrode processes at insulators.

A.D.Graves, G.J.Hills and D.Inman, *Adv. Electrochem. Electrochemical Eng.*, 4 (1966) 117. Introduction to, and review of, electrochemistry in molten salts.

J.W.Woodbury, S.H.White, M.C.Mackey, W.L.Hardy and D.B.Chang, in *Treatise on Physical Chemistry, Vol. IX B (Electrochemistry)*, Ch. 11. Topics in bio-electrochemistry.

W.F.Floyd, in *Electrical Phenomena at Interfaces* (Methuen 1951), p. 229. Electrical properties of biological membranes.

W.F.Floyd, *Modern Aspects Electrochem.*, 1 (1954) 277. Electrochemistry of nerves and muscles.

G.A.Kenney and D.C.Walker, *Electroanal. Chem.*, 5 (1971) 1. Hydrated electron in electrochemistry.

Detailed treatments of Specific Topics

Theory of Charge-Transfer Processes –
V.G.Levich, in *Treatise on Physical Chemistry, Vol. IX B (Electrochemistry)*, Ch. 12.

R.A.Marcus, *Ann. Rev. Phys. Chem.*, 15 (1964) 155.

R.Parsons, *Adv. Electrochem. Electrochemical Eng.*, 7 (1970) 177.

D.B.Matthews and J. O'M.Bockris, *Modern Aspects Electrochem.*, 6 (1971) 242.

Electrical Double-Layer –
D.M.Mohilner, *Electroanal. Chem.*, 1 (1966) 241; thorough discussion and review.

P.Delahay, *Double Layer and Electrode Kinetics* (Wiley 1965); compressed treatment with mention of numerous specific systems, comprehensive references.

C.A.Barlow, in *Treatise on Physical Chemistry, Vol. IX A (Electrochemistry)*,, Ch. 2; emphasis on aspects not discussed elsewhere.

J.E.B.Randles, *Adv. Electrochem. Electrochemical Eng.*, *3* (1963) 1; electrolyte/gas interface.

C.A.Barlow and J.R.Macdonald, *Adv. Electrochem. Electrochemical Eng.*, *6* (1967) 1; discreteness-of-charge effect.

R.Payne, *Adv. Electrochem. Electrochemical Eng.*, *7* (1970) 1; non-aqueous systems.

R.Parsons, *Adv. Electrochem. Electroohemical Eng.*, *1* (1961) 1; double-layer influence on faradaic processes.

R.S.Perkins and T.N.Anderson, *Modern Aspects Electrochem.*, *5* (1969) 203; point of zero charge — theory and experimental data.

Adsorption Processes —

B.B.Damaskin, O.A.Petrii and V.V.Batrokov, *Adsorption of Organic Compounds on Electrodes* (Plenum 1971).

P.Delahay, *Double Layer and Electrode Kinetics* (Wiley 1965).

E.Gileadi (ed.), *Electrosorption* (Plenum 1967).

Transport Processes —

V.G.Levich, *Physicochemical Hydrodynamics* (Prentice Hall 1962).

C.Wagner, *Adv. Electrochem. Electrochemical Eng.*, *2* (1962) 1.

O.Kardos and D.G.Foulke, *Adv. Electrochem. Electrochemical Eng.*, *2* (1962) 145.

A.J.Arvia and S.L.Marchiano, *Modern Aspects Electrochem.*, *6* (1971) 159.

J.Newman, *Adv. Electrochem. Electrochemical Eng.*, *5* (1967) 87.

G.J.Janz and R.D.Reeves, *Adv. Electrochem. Electrochemical Eng.*, *5* (1967) 137; in molten salts.

Solid Electrodes —

R.N.Adams, *Electrochemistry at Solid Electrodes* (Dekker 1969); restricted to inert solid electrodes, emphasis on electroanalytical view-point.

J.O'M.Bockris and G.A.Razumney, *Fundamental Aspects of Electrocrystallization* (Plenum 1967); brief survey of concepts.

H.Fischer, *Elektrolytische Abscheidung und Elektrokristallisation von Metallen* (Springer 1954); detailed discussion of many specific reactions, emphasis on practical aspects, theory now somewhat dated.

R. de Levie, *Adv. Electrochem. Electrochemical Eng.*, *6* (1967) 329; current distribution at rough and porous electrodes.

D.A.Vermilyea, *Adv. Electrochem. Electrochemical Eng.*, *3* (1963) 211; anodic films.

J. O'M. Bockris and A.R.Despic, in *Treatise on Physical Chemistry, Vol. IX B (Electrochemistry)*, Ch. 7; deposition and dissolution of metals.

M.Fleischmann and H.R.Thirsk, *Adv. Electrochem. Electrochemical Eng.*, *3* (1963) 123; electrocrystallization.

J.A.Harrison and H.R.Thirsk, *Electroanal. Chem.*, *5* (1971) 67; metal deposition.

Techniques and Methodology —

P.Delahay, *New Instrumental Methods in Electrochemistry* (Interscience 1954); remains an excellent introduction.

D.J.G.Ives and G.J.Janz, *Reference Electrodes* (Academic 1961); the indispensable classic on this subject.

J.N.Butler, *Adv. Electrochem. Electrochemical Eng.*, *7* (1970) 77; reference electrodes in aprotic solvents.

E.Yeager and J.Kuta, in *Treatise on Physical Chemistry, Vol. IX A (Electrochemistry)*, Ch. 4; up-to-date review of techniques for studying electrode reactions.

Subject Index

(Numbers in italics refer to pages where the terms are defined)

Galvanostatic, *10*
Gibbs adsorption equation, 33, 36
Ground loops, 114, 116

Half-cell potential, see Single-electrode potential
Hydration and specific adsorption, 32

Ideally polarized electrode, *9*
Indicator electrode, *7*
Inert electrolyte, *8*
Inner double-layer, 47
    capacity of 41
Inner Helmholtz layer, *32*
Inner Helmholtz plane, *32*
Integral capacity, *36*
Ionics, *2*

Langmuir isotherm, 83
Lippmann electrometer, 109
Lippmann equation, 36
Liquid-junction potentials, 37, 121

Microelectrode, *7*
Multilayer adsorption, 76

Negative exchange-current, 57
Negative rate-constant, 57
Non-faradaic current, *7*
Non-polarizable electrode, *8*

Optical studies, 126
Orientation of water molecules, 42
Oscilloscopic (oscillographic) polarography, *11*
Outer Helmholtz layer, *32*
    plane, *33*
    potential at 46
Overpotential, *8*
Overvoltage, *8*
Oxide films, 102

P.Z.C., see Potential of zero charge
Polarization, *8*
Polarography, *10*, 63
    alternating current (a.c.) *11*
    oscilloscopic (oscillographic) *11*
    pulse *11*
    radio-frequency *11*
    square-wave *11*
Potential, (usage of term) *9*
    cathodic *7*
    difference between phases 4
    effect on rate constant 16
    effect on transfer coefficient 24
    electrical *4*
    formal standard *17*
    liquid-junction 37, 121
    of hydrogen electrode 6
    of zero charge 30

Potential, rational scale of *37*
    single-electrode – see Single-electrode potential
Potential-step electrolysis, 62
Potentiostatic, *10*
Pulse polarography, *11*
Purification of solutions, 100

Radio-frequency polarography, *11*
Radiotracers, 125
Rate constant, 16, 26
    effect of potential 16
    negative 57
    significance of 26
    standard *17*
Rational scale of potential, *37*
Reaction layer for charge transfer, 26
Reference electrode, 7, 20
Relative surface-excess, *35*
    of anions 38
    of cations 38
Reorientation of adsorbed substances, 77
Reversibility, *8*, 19
Rigid double-layer, *33*; see Inner double-layer
Ring-disc electrode, 70
Rotating disc electrode, 67

Shielding, 113
Single-electrode potential, 3 ff. 27
    calculation of 5
Specific adsorption, 31, 39, 49
    and hydration 32
    of anions 31
    of cations 52, 96
Spectroscopic methods, 126
Square-wave polarography, *11*
Standard rate-constant, *17*
Static capacity, *36*
Supporting electrolyte, *8*
Surface area determination, 101
Surface concentration, 26
Surface-charge density, 36
Surface-excess concentration, 33, 34
Symmetry factor, *16*

Tafel equation, 15, 18
Tafel slope, *15*
Tensammetric wave, 74
Tensammetry, *11*
Tension, (usage of term) *9*
Three-electrode circuit, 123
Transfer coefficient, *16*, 21
    potential dependence 24
Voltage, (usage of term) *9*
Voltammetry, *11*
Voltostatic, *10*

Working electrode, *7*

131